Trailblazers for TRANSLATORS

The Chichicastenango Twelve

by

Anna Marie Dahlquist

William Carey Library

PASADENA, CALIFORNIA

Published by
William Carey Library
1705 N. Sierra Bonita Ave.
Pasadena, California 91104
818-798-0819

Library of Congress Cataloging-in-Publication Data

Dahlquist, Anna Marie, 1939-
   Trailblazers for translators : the Chichicastenango twelve
/ Anna Marie Dahlquist
      p.   cm.
   Includes bibliographical references.
   ISBN 0-87808-205-0 (paperback)
   1. Indians of Central America—Guatemala—Missions.
2. Indians—Missions. 3. Bible. N.T.—Translating. 4. Indians of Central America—Guatemala—Languages—
Translating. 5. Indians—Languages—Translating. I. Title.
F1465.3.M57D34 1992
266'.0089'9707281—dc20   91-65732
                                                              CIP

Cover Illustration and design by Mary Lou Totten

Acknowledgments

I wish to thank the many people who helped me research and write this book. Special appreciation goes to Dr. Ralph Winter and his wife Roberta for seeing the need of such a study and encouraging me to tell the story. Thanks also to those persons who provided access to the Dinwiddie, Legters, Townsend, Robinson and Treichler correspondence from the 1920s: Dr. Wilkins Winn, Jeanne Olson, Calvin Hibbard, Hugh Steven, Brainerd Legters, William Raws, and my mother Pauline Burgess Sywulka.

I am also grateful to the following people who checked the manuscript for historical accuracy and provided valuable constructive criticism: Dr. Ralph Winter, Dr. David Scotchmer, Hugh Steven, and my father Edward Sywulka.

Finally, thanks to my husband Richard and our daughters Ruth and Elizabeth for their patience and support during the many hours of research and writing.

Contents

Foreword

What a useful book Anna Marie Dahlquist has put together for us. What a worthwhile task to assemble the histories, the correspondence and the settings of the men God was leading to be part of a new awakening for the indigenous peoples of the world. What deftness of skill she applied to weave it all together—or rather discover God's weaving—and put it on display for our approval and wonder.

Obviously 1921 was an auspicious year. For the twelve it was a peak of growing discontent with a traditional approach that proclaimed the "Indian problem" solved, or solvable, through eventual assimilation into national languages and cultures. The evidence to those who looked more closely, however, was otherwise. And it still is.

Not that the prospect of addressing the challenge head on wasn't staggering. Language obstacles are formidable, especially when alphabets are non-existent, and there are no textbooks to guide in their learning. With odd sounds and complex constructions they serve as shrouds concealing mysteries of culture and religion and the value of persons.

But these were people of value even if the traditionalists were too busy, too overwhelmed with other work, to see it. Obviously it would take a new generation to approach the challenge, one idealistic and naive to the impossibilities.

They were called visionaries, though the word was a pejorative. They were products of yet earlier seers who had begun to preach the evangelization of all the peoples on the earth in their generation. These young men knew that had to include the Indians.

It is symbolic that the meeting which brought the twelve young disciples together in 1921 took place in Chichicastenango. It's a town known even today for public performance of ancient rites—dark priests chanting, swinging incense on the steps of a church that is Catholic only in name, animals sacrificed in the high places to appease spirits of the earth, people going into debt paying such shamans to cure their ailments or curse their enemies. It's as though the volcanic ground still seethes with vapors of occult origin. The customs persist even with a certain pride as if to say, "This is Indian, this is Mayan, this is us!"

It is also deception, only in detail different from all the rest from which Christ came to save. His word sets men free everywhere. But until that word is put into my own language, it's everywhere but here. It all just seems like some outsider's religion. It's shrouded in mystery.

Set in one's own language, however, it's all so right and natural and Christ is one of us indeed.

That's what the twelve saw. And they had the tenacity, the energy, the faith to attempt to finish it in their generation. It was an audacious thought. What they couldn't know was how big the job was, how many mountains loomed beyond the peaks they could see on the ascent. The earth has vastly more languages than anyone imagined in 1921.

God certainly knew what they didn't—that not enough earnest believers would turn out to finish the job in that generation. Still He led them to start. And it wasn't the first time God started a movement with men numbering twelve. For us it's fortunate the workers were too few; it gives us a chance to enter in. Who knows, maybe it will be our generation that will finish the task. It's worth a try, and worth all the energy and faith and visionary outlook we, under God, can muster.

The weaving is still in the making. These pages display the beginnings.

Hyatt Moore
Director
Wycliffe Bible Translators, USA

Publisher's Foreword

From time to time the Publisher of a book will add a "Publisher's Foreword" in order to allow readers to understand some of the special circumstances behind the publishing of a book. This is a book that was commissioned by the publisher because of the global significance of a certain train of events that focused in a small gathering in a mountain town in Guatemala in January of 1921. Probably the leading character in that event was Paul Burgess, although a much younger man who was present was eventually the chief implementer of the ideas hatched there. We asked Burgess's granddaughter, Anna Marie Dahlquist, to write this story for the general public. She is a professional writer who had at that time had already done research in the process of writing her excellent biography* *Burgess of Guatemala*— the Paul Burgess who was the most experienced person at the meeting. We are so very grateful that she was willing to take on this more specific study of this unusual but little-noticed meeting off in the mountains of Guatemala at Chichicastenango.

Why was this meeting so important? Because it was to have literally an earthshaking impact. As a result of it and its fascinating fallout, probably more of the minority peoples of this planet have been exposed to the Bible than can be attributed to any other meeting ever held in modern times. Thousands of tribal peoples have gained friendly, permanent ties with the larger world through the many streams of influence of this one meeting.

But there is much more to this story than that meeting. That small group of missionaries is here dubbed "The Chichicastenango Twelve." Those individuals were a remarkably creative and competent team during that three day meeting, deriving as they did from diverse backgrounds and different missions. The minutes of that unusual event, here given in complete form (Appendix A), reveal truly amazing insight, heartfelt concern and practical and legal knowledge. The resulting bylaws of a new mission agency are themselves a very impressive achievement.

---

*For information write to Anna Marie Dahlquist, 1643 Winter Street, Kingsburg, CA 93631, or Email: adahlquist@aol.com

Trailblazers for Translators

Several unusually wise traits of the proposed organization are pointed out in the diagrams of Appendix B. Most of these concepts were incorporated years later into another agency, the Wycliffe Bible Translators, which essentially replaced this early, embryonic structure that, unfortunately, was to be stillborn. William Cameron Townsend is the one known today better than any of the rest. His personality, as he matured, displayed a remarkable ability to get along with people, to get close to very important leaders in a number of countries and to interpret the challenge of the native tongues of smaller peoples not only to such national leaders but also to Bible believing church people who would provide the all-important human and financial resources for what would be a major, global vision. His greatest contribution is not that he originated the idea that taking tribal languages seriously is crucial to mission efforts, but that he was able to listen closely enough to learn that fact from older leaders, and then with a sustained drive that lasted over half a century, build that idea into a global enterprise. The Wycliffe Bible Translators organization has never set out to do the job by itself. It has from the beginning generously trained thousands of workers who have seeded many other organizations and created parallel structures as well. That is what Townsend wanted.

What kind of a background contributed to that astonishing accomplishment? This book tells a heretofore untold story of how problems and setbacks, small and large, do not always stop those people who possess an inner Spirit-born determination. Obstacles and even tragedies can strengthen them.

While this book is a much larger story than that of Townsend, it provides a highly important glimpse into a period earlier in his life, years before the beginnings of what is now known as Wycliffe Bible Translators. Most of all it describes the human origin of a vast global drive to reach out in love to the smallest human pockets on this planet. This phenomenon today, in its larger dimensions, is often referred to as "the Unreached Peoples Movement," and it is now center stage in the finishing of the Task. All who today participate in that larger movement will be nourished and challenged by this beautifully written book—for which we must all be grateful to Anna Marie Dahlquist!

Ralph D. Winter
for the William Carey Library
Pasadena, California, USA
July 1995

PREFACE

TRACING THE ROOTS

By 1990, over 6,000 Wycliffe Bible Translators around the world were working to give ethnic minorities the New Testament in their own tongues. The organization is gaining hundreds of new recruits a year. No other mission society is growing as fast. Furthermore, scores of translators trained by the Summer Institute of Linguistics (SIL), working under other agencies, are also translating the New Testament for minority language groups.

What are the roots of this Bible translation team effort, which is perhaps the greatest missionary thrust of the twentieth century? The first "Camp Wycliffe" was begun by L. L. Legters and William Cameron Townsend in Sulphur Springs, Arkansas, in 1934. However, the origins of the Bible translation movement go back much further.

Tracing the roots of this movement has not been unlike tracing a family tree. Sam Jones may say that he is part Welsh, part Irish, part German, and part Cherokee. He may find great fascination in tracing each of these family lines. But when he comes to write down his genealogy, where does he begin? Does he start with himself and go backwards? Or does he begin with some immigrant ancestor and trace only one line at a time? He may feel rather confused.

1

My problem is similar to that of Sam Jones. The modern Bible translation movement has roots in many other movements. Which of these "family lines" should I trace?

One can say that the Bible translation movement grew out of the Student Volunteer Movement. It is equally true that it grew out of the Victorious Life Movement. One could even say that it is an offshoot of the Central American Mission founded by C. I. Scofield of reference Bible fame, since Cameron Townsend pioneered under that agency, and then broke off to establish his own work.

The Student Volunteer Movement itself could be said, perhaps, to have derived significantly from the zest and momentum of the already global YMCA. Moreover, Ralph Winter has conjectured that most or perhaps all of the 100 original volunteers came out of local churches involved in the highly mission-minded International Society of Christian Endeavor, which in turn owes its origin and rapid proliferation to the already enormous Women's Missionary Society movement!

What is abundantly clear is that the Bible translation movement of the twentieth century is not simply the brainchild of one man. Cameron Townsend was greatly used by God, and without his remarkable foresight, persistence and diplomacy, the Summer Institute of Linguistics and the Wycliffe Bible Translators would never have become what they are today. Nevertheless, the importance of the vision of those who worked with Townsend in the early days—Robinson, Dinwiddie, Legters, Burgess and others—should not be underestimated.

These men and others—twelve persons in all—converged on January 23, 1921, in the highland city of Chichicastenango, Guatemala. While Quiché witch doctors swung their incense-filled censers on the steps of the ancient Santo Tomás cathedral, unhindered and unevangelized by Rossbach, the benign Catholic prelate, the twelve missionaries held an "Indian Conference" which was to change the course of mission history.

Prior to this conference, there had been isolated attempts at translating the Bible for tribal peoples in Latin America. The Moravians had made a good beginning with evangelism and Bible translation among the Miskito Indians of Nicaragua. But that was only one agency, and only one tribe. Never before had a group of men and women from different agencies and denominational backgrounds banded together in a team, forming an organization for the express purpose of evangelizing tribal groups and translating God's Word into their unwritten languages. It was a first in mission history.

Before we look at these twelve persons and their work more closely, let us observe three of their spiritual and missiological "ancestral lines."

THE BIBLE SOCIETIES

The British and Foreign Bible Society, founded in 1804, was one of the earliest organizations to advocate Bible translation for tribal peoples. Their agents not only distributed Spanish Scriptures in Central America, but also urged the existing missions (such as the Baptists in Belize and the Moravians in Nicaragua) to translate God's Word into the Indian tongues.

In 1892 Rev. F. de P. Castells was appointed by the British and Foreign Bible Society to head up its work in Central America. He immediately began to urge translations for the Mayas and for other tribes, but found no support from the missionaries with whom he came in contact. The 1902 British and Foreign Bible Society *Annual Report* says of him: "His efforts were at first severely criticized. The languages of these tribes were not thought worthy of Bible translation. It was declared that any version produced must needs prove utterly useless. The Indians were considered too ignorant, and the Society and its Agent were pronounced visionaries."

In spite of opposition from the established missions, Castells commissioned translations of Scripture portions into Yucatec Maya and into Carib. In 1897, at the urging of Presbyterian pi-

3

oneer Edward Haymaker, he also commissioned a translation of the Gospel of Mark into Quiché. This work was undertaken by Felipe Silva, a Catholic professor of Mayan languages at San Carlos University in Guatemala City. Castells himself supervised the translation, which was published in 1898. A second edition was published the following year and a third in 1902. The total of the three editions amounted to 7,000 copies which were distributed by the Bible Society colporteurs.

Castells himself undertook to translate Mark's Gospel into Cakchiquel. This translation was published in 1902 in a 2,000-copy edition.

Castells was outspoken about the need for Bible translation among the Indians of Latin America. At the Ecumenical Missionary Conference held at New York in 1900 he sought to disprove two widely-held myths: namely, that the Indians of Latin America could be reached through the Spanish Scriptures, and that, being nominally Catholic, they had already been adequately evangelized.

The American Bible Society was established in Philadelphia in 1808. It opened its first South American agency in Argentina in 1864, and in 1892 it sent Rev. Francisco Penzotti, an Argentine Methodist, to Guatemala to open an agency there. A bold and tireless pioneer, Penzotti organized a house-to-house colportage system which literally covered the whole country. The American Bible Society also participated in the 1894-1896 Arthington Survey (see Chapter Eight) which led to a renewed interest in the many unevangelized tribes of Central America.

Having two different Bible societies working in the same country seemed an unnecessary duplication of effort, so in 1912 the British and Foreign Bible Society turned all of its work over to the American Bible Society. In time both Rev. Castells and Rev. Penzotti left Guatemala, and the work of Scripture distribution was left largely in the hands of individual colporteurs and missionaries.

The early work of the Bible societies is important in un-

4

derstanding the contribution to Bible translation made by "The Chichicastenango Twelve." The Bible societies laid the foundation upon which subsequent translation efforts were built. Although Castells was not trained and skilled as a linguist, he had a great vision for Bible translation. He understood the importance of reaching tribal peoples in their mother tongue in an age when the vast majority of missionaries were opposed to this concept. Townsend, Burgess, Legters and others followed in this tradition when they too emphasized the need of vernacular Scriptures for the Indians, despite the opposition of missionary leaders.

THE STUDENT VOLUNTEER MOVEMENT

In 1886, 250 college students gathered at Mount Hermon, Massachussetts, at a conference called by evangelist D. L. Moody. Before the conference was over, 100 of them had signed a little card designed by a young missions enthusiast named Robert Wilder. The pledge card stated simply, "God helping me, I purpose to be a foreign missionary."

One of the hundred delegates who signed that card was John R. Mott. He later became a great missionary statesman, traveling to colleges and seminaries all over the country and awakening a burning missionary zeal wherever he went. More than any other man, Mott was responsible for the phenomenal organizational growth of the Student Volunteer Movement which was born at Mt. Hermon in 1886. Sweeping the campuses of America during the early third of the twentieth century, this movement provided literally thousands of recruits for more than fifty mission-sending agencies, which in turn thrust these young volunteers out into the far corners of the earth in an unparalleled missionary advance.

The watchword of the Student Volunteer Movement was "The Evangelization of the World in this Generation." The slogan caught fire all across the nation as Robert Wilder, John R. Mott, Robert Speer, and others toured the campuses of the continent.

The influence of the Student Volunteer Movement upon the twelve people who met at Chichicastenango in 1921 can be sensed in their resolve to reach the Indians for Christ "in this generation." Chapter One will explore the background of some of those who met in that historic conference, and the influence of the Student Volunteer Movement will be seen particularly in the lives of Burgess and Townsend.

THE VICTORIOUS LIFE MOVEMENT

In 1906 a missionary to India organized the New Wilmington Missionary Conference in western Pennsylvania, a ministry which sprang out of the revival which had come to India some time before. The New Wilmington meetings stressed Bible study, prayer, and spiritual growth as well as mission. It was here in 1910 that Charles Trumbull, renowned editor of *The Sunday School Times*, entered into a "transforming experience" as he realized that the secret of the Christian life is found in the indwelling presence of Christ.

A year later, in 1911, young Robert McQuilkin, hungering for victory in his Christian life, heard Trumbull speak at New Wilmington, prayed with him, and then entered into a life of surrender and trust in Christ.

The following year McQuilkin moved to Philadelphia to work for *The Sunday School Times*. He and his bride began an informal prayer group in their home, which led to the organization of a Victorious Life Conference, separate from that held in New Wilmington. Its first meetings were held in Oxford, Pennsylvania, on July 19-23, 1913, the exact dates of the annual Keswick Convention held in England. Later this "American Keswick" moved to Princeton, then to Long Island, and finally to its present location at Keswick Grove, New Jersey.

The Victorious Life Testimony, an organization which grew out of McQuilkin's prayer group and conference, continued to function out of Philadelphia, with J. Harvey Borton as

6

chairman, B. F. Culp as treasurer, and Charles Trumbull as head of the editorial and literature department. Two men served as "secretaries" of the organization: Robert McQuilkin and Howard Dinwiddie. Both engaged in extensive conference ministry, speaking about the Victorious Christian Life in meetings throughout the country. Later McQuilkin moved to South Carolina and became the founder and first president of Columbia Bible College, a school which still emphasizes the Victorious Christian Life and which has sent out thousands of missionaries, hundreds of them Bible translators, since its beginning in 1923.

In 1919, while the Keswick conferences were still being held on Long Island, a pastor and former missionary named L. L. Legters attended the meetings in search of victory over his triple besetting sins: tobacco, hot temper, and worry. Through McQuilkin's messages he learned the secret of surrender and trust. Here, too, Legters met Howard Dinwiddie, and in his enthusiasm over his new-found secret of victory, Legters joined Dinwiddie in holding Victorious Life Conferences throughout the United States.

In late 1920 Dinwiddie was sent to Guatemala to hold Victorious Life meetings for the missionaries. There he met both Cameron Townsend and Paul Burgess, and as he traveled and conversed with them, he came to share their deep burden for the Indians. Dinwiddie knew that his friend Legters also shared this burden, and so he told Townsend and Burgess: "I must bring Mr. Legters here. He has worked among the Indians and understands them."

And so Dinwiddie, man of action, cabled Legters to join him at an "Indian Conference" in Guatemala. Although Legters had a wife who was very ill at that time, he responded to the cable and met with eleven other concerned persons at the Chichicastenango Conference.

Both Legters and Dinwiddie came to Guatemala primarily to preach the Victorious Life. Organizing a new mission to reach the Indians was probably not part of their original objective. But at the Chichicastenango Conference, they did just that. And the organization they formed, known familiarly as "The Protestant Indian League" or more officially as "The Latin American Indian Mission," was a direct forebear of Wycliffe Bible Translators.

Before exploring what actually happened at the Chichicastenango Conference, let us take a peek at the lives of the key figures in that meeting. What was the burden they shared, and how had the Lord worked to bring them together?

1

A BURDEN IS SHARED

WILLIAM CAMERON TOWNSEND
AND ELVIRA M. TOWNSEND

Young Cam Townsend, a Bible salesman working in Guatemala, got up from the dying campfire and shivered in the highland evening chill before he hung up his hammock for the night. His Cakchiquel friend and guide, whom he had nicknamed Frisco, and he had just had another long talk about the needs of the Indians.

Cam, a slender, sandy-haired youth of twenty-one, had been spending seven or eight pesos a day for his own beans and tortillas. But he learned from Frisco that many Indians did not even earn five or six pesos a day. Some coffee plantation owners paid their Indian peons only three pesos a day! How could a man support a family on that, even if all he fed them was tortillas?

Townsend's December 1917 diary reveals his concern for the economic plight of the Indians:

> With each plantation visit, I am made painfully aware of the plight of the indentured Indian. I have found thousands of highland-born Indian people who are now entrapped by the colono system. This system is virtual slavery. They have been brought to live and work year-round on the coastal plantations. The Indian borrows a small amount of money from the landowner, generally for the purpose of drinking. If he cannot pay back his debt the Indian is forced by the government to serve the lender for a certain length of time

9

each year at a small wage. Unfortunately, the Indian never seems to be able to pay off his debt. If the plantation is sold, the colono is transferred to serve the new master. Further, a colono is not allowed to leave the plantation without permission.

On some of these plantations I found stocks and whipping posts. One Indian told me of how he was whipped until he was almost unconscious. Another told how he was strung up by his thumbs and made to sit for days in the stocks unsheltered from the sun.(1)

Townsend, however, was concerned not only for the economic plight of the Indians, but also for their spiritual needs. The witch doctors had great power over the people, and few of the Catholic priests had done anything to break that power or to teach the Indians what Christianity was really all about. A veneer of Christian phrases was superimposed upon the ancient Mayan rituals, and Catholic images, in some cases, took the place of stone idols, but the Indians did not really know the gospel.

And they did not have God's Word! True, the Bible Society had published Scripture portions in Quiché and Cakchiquel. Cam himself had peddled some of these selections. But somehow the people did not seem to understand the translation any better than the Spanish Scriptures.

How very much needed to be done for the Indians! They should have the Bible in their tongue; they should have schools, hospitals, and Bible institutes! Why was it, Cameron asked himself, that these Indians had not been reached by the eighty some missionaries who were working in Central America?

Well, if no one else was reaching the Indians, he would do it! His August 30, 1918, journal entry shows his resolve:

A subject Frisco and I frequently discuss around the campfire and on the trails is the need of Frisco's own people, the Cakchiquels. When I observed the Indians in El Salvador and Honduras and saw how they suffered less oppression and had more freedom than the Indians in Guatemala, my heart burned within me for Guatemala's suffering people. And when I see how quickly Frisco

10

learned and how eager he was to follow the Lord and do his will, and how many latent possibilities there are in him and his people, I am stirred even further to recognize the need among the Cakchiquel people.

I did a survey of all the missionaries who for years have served faithfully in Guatemala, and almost none of them have seen fit to learn any of the Indian languages. This means that sixty percent of the people in this republic have no gospel witness. The reason for this is the difficulty of learning the many different languages and dialects, all of which are unwritten.

I have come to realize that it is imperative this need be surmounted in this generation and the people be reached with the message of salvation. God has given me youthful vigor, faith and a challenge. Therefore, I have decided to devote my life to the evangelization of the Indian peoples.(2)

The phrase "it is imperative this need be surmounted in this generation" shows the strong influence of the Student Volunteer Movement on Townsend.

Townsend, born in California in 1896, was raised as a Presbyterian and attended Occidental College in Los Angeles. During his sophomore year he was awakened to missions by reading the life of James Hudson Taylor, and that very year he joined the Student Volunteer Band, pledging his life to be a foreign missionary.

At a meeting sponsored by the Student Volunteers, Cam and his friend Elbert "Robbie" Robinson heard John R. Mott challenge the students to evangelize the world "in this generation."

The two young men heard God's call and in August 1917 they left for Guatemala to work as colporteurs for the Bible House of Los Angeles. Townsend still had not finished college. He had promised to work as a Bible salesman for only a year, and he did not know that the year would stretch into a lifetime of serving Bibleless peoples.

He only knew that he felt called to reach the suffering Indian people. How alone he must have felt at times as he walked the trails. Was there no other missionary who shared his deep burden for these ethnic minorities? Did no one else care about translating the Bible for them?

Perhaps he was unaware that at that very time God was placing the same burden on other hearts, and that a great awakening to the needs of the neglected tribes was dawning. One of those who shared his burden was Elvira Malmstrom, a Moody Church member who came to Guatemala to serve as stenographer for William B. Allison, senior Presbyterian missionary. When Townsend and she became engaged, Elvira wrote to Paul and Dora Burgess, who were on furlough:

> We both feel called to work among the Indians. Right now our hearts are with the Cakchiquel Indians, and we are asking the Lord to definitely direct us as to just where he would have us settle down.(3)

On July 9, 1919, Cam and Elvira were married in Guatemala City, with Allison performing the ceremony and Paul Burgess, just back from furlough, preaching the wedding sermon. The newlyweds then went on to work in Antigua, Guatemala, under the Central American Mission. Later they moved to the nearby town of San Antonio Aguas Calientes.

By December 1920, when Townsend met Dinwiddie and shared with him the great vision which God had given to him and Elvira, "the newlyweds" were already rapidly advancing in their study of Cakchiquel and were making their first attempts at Bible translation. But their hearts were still burdened, for there was so much more which needed to be done, not just for the Cakchiquels, but also for many other needy tribes. And so, when the 1921 Chichicastenango Indian Conference was convened, Cameron Townsend posed the question: "Are the present means for the evangelization of the Indian adequate?"

PAUL BURGESS AND DORA M. BURGESS

On July 3, 1917, Rev. Paul Burgess, the tall, lanky pastor of Bethel Church in Quetzaltenango, sat at his desk looking over his Spanish sermon notes. Suddenly he was interrupted by some shocking news.

He learned that a group of Quiché witch doctors had just brutally murdered five young men—two of them members of his German congregation—and had thrown their mutilated bodies into a volcano crater as a sacrifice to the spirits of the mountains. This tragedy caused Paul and his wife Dora to become more concerned than ever before for the spiritual needs of the Indians. Dora capsuled their reaction in a letter to supporters:

> Our strength is already overtaxed in looking after the 50 congregations already established. We ourselves have long desired to devote ourselves to the Indian work exclusively, if another missionary could be sent to relieve us of the Spanish work. If the death of these young men serves to call the attention of the Church to the imperative need of Indian evangelization, they will not have died in vain. Pray for these poor Indians and for us that a door may be opened by which the Gospel message of love to God and man may be brought to these people with a knowledge of a God of mercy and forgiveness, who demands not the sacrifice of human beings, but only an obedient and contrite heart.(4)

From that day on, Paul and Dora Burgess began to pray more earnestly than ever that their board would free them for Indian work. But their interest in the Indians had been awakened long before that fateful day.

Paul Burgess, born in New York State in the very year that saw the birth of the Student Volunteer Movement, was perhaps, of all the "Chichicastenango Twelve," the most typical Student Volunteer: a college graduate sent out by a denominational board.

Burgess grew up in Colorado and joined the Student Volunteer Band of Colorado College. He continued his studies—and his Student Volunteer involvement—at McCormick Seminary in Chicago. In 1909 he attended the sixth international quadrennial Student Volunteer Convention, along with some three thousand other students, representing over seven hundred schools from around the world. Here he heard John R. Mott,

Robert Speer, and other speakers who had challenged his heart earlier. Paul spoke of the convention:

> The Watchword, "The Evangelization of the World in this Generation," suggests the enormity of our task, and drives us to seek Divine Aid. It kills apathy in us and leads us to self sacrifice, and above all, it gives us a vision—for a vision we must have if we would do great things. . . . No one could attend this great convention and hear the singing of that great audience when they sang "Faith of Our Fathers" without realizing that this faith is living still. . . . And everyone, too, gained a desire for a deeper and more victorious life for himself, and for having a part in this great movement. (5)

After his marriage to Dora McLaughlin, and further studies at the Universities of Marburg and Berlin and at the Sorbonne, Burgess arrived in Guatemala in late 1913 under the Board of Foreign Missions of the Presbyterian Church (USA). Although he expected to be assigned to educational work, he was instead sent to Quezaltenango to do evangelism.

Here the Burgesses were surrounded by Quiché and Mam Indians who needed the gospel desperately, for there were only two Quiché-speaking believers in the whole province at that time. But four years passed before the terrible volcano tragedy prompted Paul and Dora to make a concerted effort to be freed from other duties so that they could devote themselves to the Indians.

Although their board did not immediately free them (they were still assigned Spanish and German work), so great was their love for the Indians that they began to learn Quiché, to translate hymns, and to organize Quiché churches even though many of their fellow missionaries were opposed to distinctively Indian work and scoffed at the idea of using tribal languages rather than teaching the Indians Spanish and assimilating them into the Spanish-speaking churches.

Burgess was not only concerned at this time for the Quiché tribe, but also for the Mam tribe, and he begged the Bible society to begin a translation into Mam. (See Chapter Seven.)

When the senior Presbyterian missionaries saw how successful his incipient Indian work was, they began to understand the value of reaching tribal peoples in their mother tongue. In 1919 Paul wrote:

> . . . Mr. Allison had always opposed distinctive work for the Indians. But when we organized the church in Cantel last Thursday with 100 charter members, he was so impressed with the strength of the Indian character that he spoke glowingly of the future of the new Church and carried off the pen with which the covenant was signed, as a souvenir.(6)

Yet Burgess was still hampered by all the Spanish and German work assigned to him. He wrote to Townsend:

> We envy you your opportunity to do some real language study. I have found it very difficult if not impossible. But we hope to have the Sullenberger family with us shortly and expect then to go after the lengua with . . . enthusiasm. . . . Did I write you that we are planning to get out a small Hymnal in Catshiquel [*sic*] before long? Have several hymns ready. If you have any suggestions send them along and by all means hymns.(7)

Burgess may have used the term "Catshiquel" to cover both the Quiché and Cakchiquel languages, as they are somewhat similar. Correspondence shows that his hymnal was used in the Cakchiquel field as well as in the Quiché territory.

But what was a small hymnbook put out on his ancient pedal press? It was a mere beginning. There was so much more that the Burgesses wanted to do for the Indians: translate the Bible; begin a Bible training school; publish the Quichés' own book of folklore—the *Popol Vuh*—and, above all, evangelize the unreached areas. And so the Burgesses too attended the Chichicastenango Conference in early 1921 with the question burning in their hearts: "What can we do for the Indian?" Since Paul Burgess was the oldest field missionary present, it was natural for him to be elected chairman and to hold a prominent role in the early days of Indian work in Guatemala.

Trailblazers for Translators

ABRAM BENJAMIN TREICHLER
AND LOUISE TREICHLER

Ben Treichler, a rough-and-tumble man with a gift for evangelism and a "very strong, far-reaching voice" which could be heard a block away when he preached, also felt a burden for the Indians of Guatemala.

Treichler grew up in Philadelphia, attended public schools, and studied the Scofield Correspondence Course. His education was very different from that of Burgess, Townsend and Robinson, for they were college men who had signed the Student Volunteer Pledge. Nevertheless, Treichler's heart was equally set on the mission field.

Ben's wife Louise, a trained stenographer, shared his missionary vision. She was older, better educated, and more refined than her husband. Yet she determined to walk the trails with him, to knock on the doors of thatched-roof homes, and to evangelize the unreached villages.

They were accepted by the Central American Mission in 1917, and already their sights were on the Indians. The *C.A.M. Bulletin* reported: "The Lord has led them to decide to go to Huehuetenango . . . and take special work among the many Indians surrounding that city."(8)

The Treichlers arrived in Guatemala in 1918, but they did not settle in Huehuetenango. Both Ben and Louise found Spanish to be difficult ("We find the language rather slow," they wrote), and Mr. Treichler, impatient to begin evangelizing, wondered whether he should devote himself to preaching in English to the railroad employees in Guatemala City.

However, the Treichlers' vision for Indian work was revived when Cameron Townsend spent a month in their home after his journey through Honduras, El Salvador and Nicaragua. They reported that he inspired them with his stories of Frisco and the spiritual harvest which was "rich for Indian work and opportunity."(9)

16

In the spring of 1919, the Treichlers joined Cameron and his fiancée Elvira on a mule-back trip to San Antonio and Santa Catarina and reported that "we saw real Indian life." The Cakchiquel Indians needed the Gospel, the doors were wide open, and so the Treichlers decided to settle in San Lucas Tolimán, a lakeside Cakchiquel village, instead of going to Huehuetenango.

When the Townsends were married, Ben Treichler provided the gold piece which became Elvira's wedding band. The two couples had much in common; they had come to the field about the same time, both husbands were about the same age, both wives were accomplished stenographers, and all four shared the vision of reaching the Cakchiquel people.

But even the Spanish language still did not come easily. When Treichler was asked to present a message on prayer, he had to have help in translating his English message into Spanish. Then, stumbling along, he was able to read the translated message aloud.

By October 1919, the Treichlers had settled in San Lucas. They wrote: "How we wish we might show you around San Lucas and Sololá, for we are well nigh bereft of words to describe the needs."

They went on to ask prayer for their language study, "which we feel the most important, especially as here we find a dialect quite corrupt in the Spanish. Pray for at least one Christian Indian who can speak the aboriginal as well as Spanish and help as native worker."(10)

Less than a year later, the Treichlers had moved to Chichicastenango to take over a work begun by Dr. C. Secord, a Brethren missionary who had left the field under less than ideal conditions. He had gotten involved in politics, siding with the unpopular and demented dictator Estrada Cabrera. When Cabrera fell in 1920, Secord found it wise to leave Guatemala.

In Chichicastenango, an ancient Quiché city, the Treichlers were again surrounded by Indians with colorful costumes and gutteral speech, just as they had been in the Cakchiquel village of San Lucas Tolimán. Their vision for the Indians was enlarged as they listened to Howard Dinwiddie's messages in November and December 1920. First they heard him at the general missionary conference in Guatemala City. They heard him again in Quezaltenango, where they stayed with Miss Ella Williams while attending the Dinwiddie meetings in that city. Then they heard him a third time when he held a week of meetings with them in Chichicastenango in early December. So entranced were they by his messages and by the fact that he shared their burden for Guatemala's Indians, that they traveled to San Antonio to hear him a fourth time, at the conference which he and Legters held around Christmas time there. And lastly, they had Dinwiddie and Legters in their own home in Chichicastenango for the historic "Conference on the Evangelization of the Latin American Indians" which was held January 23-25, 1921.

All that November and December, the missionaries who had a burden for the Indians were sharing it with Dinwiddie. That led to Dinwiddie's inviting Legters to join him, and thus the plans for the Chichicastenango Indian Conference began to crystallize. The Treichlers played an important part in those plans, for they issued the invitations and hosted the delegates.

Their invitation to Paul and Dora Burgess stated:

> We have just received word that Mr. Dinwiddie and Mr. Legters wish to meet you and Townsends and Robinsons and ourselves in a conference, beginning January 22nd here in Chichicastenango. . . . We trust that nothing will prevent your coming to us on the 22nd. . . . We hope you will make every effort to be with us from the 22nd to the 26th. We feel that perhaps nothing is quite so important (nor so neglected at present) as the Latin American Indians, and we do want to be used in their evangelization.(11)

At that conference, convened by the Treichlers at the request of Dinwiddie and Legters, twelve individuals would share their burden, not only for Indian evangelism, but also for Bible translation.

HOWARD BROOKE DINWIDDIE

Howard B. Dinwiddie, a relative of the famous colonial governor who bore the same surname, was born in Virginia in 1877. His father was a godly Presbyterian minister who had participated with Dr. C. I. Scofield in prophetic conferences and thus was familiar with the work of the Central American Mission.

Young Dinwiddie studied at the University of Virginia, and we may assume that he was influenced by the Student Volunteer Movement at that time. In 1901 he married Maude Hasbrouk, and in 1903 he took a well-paying position as general inspector of New York City's public charities. However, his profound interest in missions and Bible teaching led him to devote most of his free time to promoting the Victorious Christian Life and the work of overseas missions.

In 1917, although he had three growing children to support, Dinwiddie resigned as inspector of charities in order to "live by faith" and serve full time as secretary of the Africa Inland Mission. His heart was one with the field missionaries of that agency, but when petty controversies and personality conflicts plagued the board, Dinwiddie resigned. In 1919 he was appointed secretary of the Victorious Life Testimony.

In the fall of 1920, the Victorious Life Testimony decided to send W. H. Griffith-Thomas and Charles Trumbull to the Far East to hold Victorious Life Conferences with missionaries and nationals there. At the same time, Dinwiddie was sent to Guatemala for a three-month trip, with the same purpose. James Hayter, a Presbyterian missionary, arranged his itinerary.

After holding general meetings in Guatemala City, Dinwiddie left for the Burgess home in Quezaltenango, where he held a conference on November 11-14. At Hayter's request, Burgess had sent out letters of invitation to other missionaries to attend these "deeper life" meetings. The Treichlers responded, and as has been noted, they were housed in the home of

Ella Williams. Another couple who attended the Quezaltenango meetings were Mr. and Mrs. Albert Hines, Pentecostal missionaries stationed at nearby Totonicapán.

Dinwiddie held meetings both for the small group of missionaries and also for the national believers. Everywhere he looked, there were Indians. As Dinwiddie heard Treichler tell of the hold of the witch doctors over the people of Chichicastenango, and as he listened to the story of the volcano massacre from the lips of Burgess, his heart was stirred.

These Indians must be reached, and they must be reached *in this generation!* Already Dinwiddie had found his heart knit to that of Burgess, Treichler and Townsend in a burden and vision for the tribal peoples of Latin America. But there was one more man whose heart was already in Indian work and who needed to share the vision of the small band of missionaries who cared about Guatemala's Indians. Dinwiddie decided to cable his friend Legters and ask him to join this band in a conference.

After holding meetings in Chichicastenango in early December, and after further discussion with the Treichlers about the tremendous needs and wonderful opportunities among the Indians, Dinwiddie returned to Guatemala City on December 14 and wrote to Burgess:

> I have just arrived in the city and leave early tomorrow for Zacapa. I must drop you at least a line to tell you that the Rev. L. L. Legters of Bishopville, South Carolina, the Presbyterian minister of whom I spoke to you as so deeply interested in the Indians, has cabled me that he is sailing on the 17th. This should bring him into Puerto Barrios early next week. I plan to bring him to Guatemala on the way to the Indian Conference at San Antonio to which all missionaries interested in the Indians especially (including yourself and wife) are cordially invited as well as the Indian workers and believers. This conference is to be Dec. 24, 25, 26.(12)

Dinwiddie then inquired as to when Burgess would be able to show Legters the Indian area around Quezaltenango, and closed his letter with "Yours for the Indians for Christ."

Burgess had four small daughters, so in spite of his longing to meet Legters and share his burden with this man who already knew and cared so much about tribal evangelism, he answered Dinwiddie:

> I want to attend that Indian conference the worst way and was going to let everything drop to do it but my wife put her foot down and said that not even to attend an Indian Conference should I leave the children without their papa on Christmas.
>
> It is fine to know that Mr. Legters is coming to visit us here in his study of the Indian problem in Central America. If he would like to see the Indian as he is, I will be glad to take him around this field for about two weeks beginning January 1st.(13)

And so Dinwiddie had to wait until after the San Antonio conference to get all the Indian-minded missionaries together. And it was at Chichicastenango that they convened.

LEONARD LIVINGSTON LEGTERS

L. L. Legters held Dinwiddie's cable in his hand, and looked down at his sick wife with a puzzled expression. "How can I leave you at this time, my dear?" he asked.

Mrs. Legters looked up from her sick bed. "God will take care of me," she replied bravely. "I'm just as anxious as you are to see those Central American Indians reached for Christ. Go ahead and make the trip!"

Rev. Legters had a long history of interest in Indian evangelism. He was born in 1873 in upstate New York, the son of a strong-willed Dutch farmer. Proud of his ancestry, Legters was able to preach in Dutch as well as in English, and realized early in life the importance of reaching people in their mother tongue.

He was twenty-one before he left his father's farm to attend Hope College in Michigan. There was a strong missionary emphasis at Hope, a school which sent delegates to the Student Volunteer Quadrennials. The young men from Hope who attended the 1898 Quadrennial at Cleveland challenged Legters and other students with their reports in meetings and their articles in the school magazine, *The Anchor*. Furloughing missionaries spoke regularly to the student body, and Legters was deeply stirred in his senior year as he heard John G. Paton make a strong appeal for volunteers for worldwide evangelism.

After graduating from Hope in 1900, and from New Brunswick Seminary in 1903 (both Dutch Reformed schools), Legters became a missionary to the Comanches and Apaches in Oklahoma, serving under the Dutch Reformed Board. Here he met his wife, who was also in Indian work, and the young couple worked alongside Dr. and Mrs. Walter Roe, missionaries who were equally enthusiastic about Indian evangelism.

Even while working in Oklahoma, Legters had a vision for the Indians of Latin America, and he began to dream of training North American Indians to serve as missionaries to the tribes of Central and South America.

From Oklahoma, Mr. and Mrs. Legters and their baby David Brainerd were transferred to California to begin Indian work among the tribes there. But a disagreement arose, and L. L. Legters left the Dutch Reformed Church and took a Southern Presbyterian pastorate in South Carolina in 1912.

One of the problems with the Dutch Reformed Church was that they did not allow their missionaries to learn the tribal languages, for the prevailing opinion at that time was that the Indians should learn English and forget their native tongues. While working with the Comanches and Apaches (Legters even had the distinction of conducting the funeral for the famed Geronimo), Leonard realized the people were simply not understanding the gospel message when he preached to them in English. Thus he circumvented the mission's unreasonable requirement by preaching effectively to his congregation in sign language. Forever after, his preaching was vivid and dramatic as he "acted out" the points of his message.

When Legters arrived in Guatemala he already knew the importance of reaching Indians in their own languages. He began his ministry there by joining Dinwiddie, the Townsends, the Robinsons, the Treichlers and a large group of Indian believers at the Christmas conference in San Antonio. Then Legters moved on to Chichicastenango to meet with the eleven other persons who shared his burden.

THE OTHER MEMBERS OF
THE "CHICHICASTENANGO TWELVE"

William Elbert Robinson

"Robbie," although ten years older than Cam Townsend, was nevertheless his best friend. The two had been active in the Student Volunteer Band at Occidental College, where Robbie was also president of the Y.M.C.A. Together they sailed out of San Francisco in late 1917, bound for Guatemala to work as salesmen for the Bible House in Los Angeles. After working in Guatemala for less than a year, in a territory separate from that covered by Townsend, Robinson returned to the United States in answer to the army's draft call. On his way back to the U.S., he stopped for a visit with Cameron, and the two men celebrated with a feast of pork, rice and *tamales*.

Only a few months later, the war ended. Robinson, however, did not return to Guatemala for another two years. He stayed in the United States to finish his degree at Occidental College and to be ordained as a Baptist minister. Then, in late 1920, he returned to Guatemala with a bride, Genevieve, to work under the Central American Mission.

Ben and Louise Treichler traveled to the Pacific port of San José to meet the young couple and bring them to their new station, the beautiful lakeside village of Panajachel, where brightly dressed Cakchiquel Indians paddled canoes, bartered in crowded market places . . . and consulted witch doctors in the steep, foreboding caves that overlook placid Lake Atitlán.

Robinson had great plans for building a home where Indians would feel welcome, a chapel where they could worship, a Bible school where Indian leaders could be trained, and a launch that could be used for reaching other lakeside villages with the gospel. Leaving his bride for a few days he too set off for Chichicastenango in early 1921 to share the burden of the unreached tribes with his buddy Cam and with others of like mind.

Herbert W. Toms and Mary H. Toms

Herbert Toms grew up as a missionary's son in Huehuetenango, Guatemala. He began his work there as a single missionary in 1911, and then in 1915 he brought a bride, Mary Hogue, to the field. Together they worked under the Central American Mission, side by side with Herbert's parents, Mr. and Mrs. Frank Toms, who had established a school and a church in Huehuetenango and were reaching the upper classes in that city.

Both Frank and Herbert Toms were interested in the many Indian tribes found in the province of Huehuetenango. Some Mam Indians are reported to have accepted Christ as early as 1905. In 1916, after making a trip into Indian territory with his son, the elder Toms wrote: "We are rejoiced to see some of the Indians manifesting interest. Some, we trust, have already accepted the truth."(14)

Herbert himself had made no effort, as far as we know, to learn any of the tribal languages found in the department of Huehuetenango. Still, he was deeply concerned about the spiritual condition of the Indians. As a result, he and his wife both attended the Chichicastenango Conference.

Ella Williams

Miss Williams was a curly-haired, musically talented young school teacher who was sent to Guatemala under the

Presbyterian board in 1917. Together with Miss Eleanor Morrison, she taught at the La Patria Girls' School in Quezaltenango. Although her work was with the Spanish-speaking population, she came in daily contact with the Quiché Indians and felt drawn to them. Close association with the Burgesses, as well as having the Treichlers as guests in her home, doubtless quickened her zeal for the Indians. It was her dream to leave the Spanish La Patria School and to begin a separate school exclusively for Indians. With this dream burning in her heart, she also came to Chichicastenango in January 1921.

2

A VISION IS BORN

The "Chichicastenango Twelve" convened on January 23, 1921, their hearts united in prayer and in an intense desire to evangelize Guatemala's tribes and to give them God's Word in their own tongue. They were all young, they were all enthusiastic, and they all believed that the tribes should be reached "in this generation."

Dinwiddie's correspondence reveals he was a man of prayer, and that he made no decisions without praying much first. We can imagine, therefore, that before the official business took place, they prayed about the needs of the Indians and about the missionaries' need for wisdom and guidance. Every great movement of God is born in prayer, and the Chichicastenango conference was no exception.

Even before the conference, the missionaries had discussed the Indian problem at length with one another. They were unanimous in feeling that the mission boards were not doing an adequate job of reaching the indigenous peoples.

The only three Central American tribes with organized groups of believers who worshipped in their mother tongue were the Miskitos of Nicaragua and the Quichés and the Cakchiquels of Guatemala. Little was being done for the Mams, the Conobs, and many other tribes within Guatemala. The missionaries were not sure exactly how many tribes there were in Central America, but the Arthington Survey had named thirty-one.

26

That meant that at least twenty-eight groups in Central America were still unreached!

The missionaries agreed that neither the Central American Mission nor the Presbyterian board was providing adequate funds, personnel, nor encouragement for Indian evangelism. For the Spanish-speaking third of Guatemala's population there were chapels, schools, dispensaries, literature, and paid pastors as well as missionaries. But for the non-Spanish-speaking two-thirds of the country, there was no provision in the budget of either agency. There were no board-sponsored Indian schools, no paid Indian evangelists, and no teams of missionaries specifically assigned to Bible translation. In fact, some board members, such as R. D. Smith of the Central American Mission, were strongly opposed to the very idea of Bible translation and most felt, "Let the Indians learn Spanish, read the Spanish Bible, and take part in Spanish church services."

And so, the Chichicastenango Twelve agreed that since the established agencies were not meeting the needs of the Indians, a new organization was needed for the tribes.

This new organization, formed not to compete with existing boards but rather to cooperate fully with them, was called The Latin American Indian Mission or the L.A.I.M. (The term "Protestant Indian League," used in the biography *Burgess of Guatemala*, is a familiar term and not the official title.)

The minutes of this organization have recently come to light through the kindness of Brainerd Legters. In order for the student of mission history to have a clear view of what transpired at the Chichicastenango Conference, the minutes will be reproduced as follows:

January 23rd, 1921

In response to a call sent out to the following missionaries urging them to meet Mr. H. B. Dinwiddie and Mr. Legters at Chichicastenango, all assembled in the home of A. B. Treichler: Mr. and Mrs. Paul Burgess, Mr. and Mrs. Herbert W. Toms, Mr. and Mrs. W. Cameron Townsend, Mr. William E. Robinson, Mr. and Mrs. Treichler, and Miss Williams.

Mr. Robinson offered a prayer for definite blessing and guidance from God in the conference to which we had been called to consider the best way to evangelize the Indians.

Mr. Townsend then stated [concerning] the utterly neglected condition of 3,000,000 Indians in Mexico; 30,000,000 Indians in South America besides the great number of Guatemalan Indians and those of the other Central American republics, that God had reminded him of Psalm 119:126—"It is time for Jehovah to work" in the evangelization of all the Indians of all Latin America in this generation and that this conference should consider first—The Local Problem, and second—The Latin American Problem.

On motion of Mr. Robinson, Mr. Burgess was appointed Chairman of the Conference. Unanimously carried.

On motion of Mr. Townsend, Mrs. Treichler was appointed secretary of the Conference.

Thereupon it was decided, on motion of Mr. Dinwiddie, that it is the sense of the meeting that the Indian problem be discussed freely and that the members of the Conference make suggestions to clarify our understanding of the Indian need and that we undertake to discuss these phases of the work in their order of importance. Unanimously carried.

Mr. Townsend presented for discussion the question: Can the Indians of Guatemala be evangelized in this generation according to the present methods?

Mr. Dinwiddie offered a prayer for a definite recognition of the Lord's will by all the members of the Conference.

The Chairman spoke of the work already established among the Indians here in Guatemala and the stamp of the Lord's blessing upon it and asked for suggestions as to methods of procedure.

Mr. Dinwiddie presented for comparison the following figures: With about 10,000 Ladino [Spanish-speaking] believers the average arrives at about twenty to one, as compared with the Indian population. He also stated the elements in this situation: the retiring nature of the Indians; that Indians usually enter Ladino congregations mainly with an idea of becoming Ladino themselves; the military service as a factor in the disintegration of the Indian civilization. As an argument for the plan to evangelize the Indians in their own tongues, Mr. Dinwiddie stated that the trade language of Africa (where there are hundreds of tribal languages) is of no use in evangelizing.

28

Then followed discussion as to the inadequacy of Indian languages to express all religious thought. Mr. Burgess argued in favor of putting the Scriptures in the Indian languages.

Mr. Dinwiddie asked if any people had ever been evangelized except in their own tongue, which the meeting were forced to answer negatively.

Mr. Legters then stated that in order to know God's will we have only to look at what God is doing already.

Mr. Dinwiddie mentioned the rule of the British Government which compels all of its officials in India to study the literature and home life and lore of the natives. A British Army officer visiting in Mexico was impressed and shocked by the imposition inflicted by the Spanish people upon the Indians and stated that the Mexicans will never manage their Indian population by their present methods.

Mr. Burgess suggested the importance of guarding against political trouble in doing Indian work.

Mr. Townsend suggested translations with parallel readings in Spanish and Indian.

Mr. Legters called attention to the fact that the only way to reach this generation of Indians is in their own tongues.

Mr. Toms asked if a translation of the Bible for the San Antonio Indians would serve for other Cachequels [*sic*].

Mr. Townsend replied that it would only serve for 150,000 Cachequels [*sic*].

Mr. Toms raised the question as to whether the best way to reach Indians is to translate the Bible into the Indian languages or to reach them through Spanish-speaking Indians.

Mr. Legters suggested that the Indians have not the training to read a Spanish Bible and understand it clearly, because of their limited knowledge of Spanish.

Mr. Legters asked for prayer as to the Lord's will about the Indians of this generation having the Gospel in their own tongue. Mr. Legters led in this prayer.

Mr. Toms raised the question of the present translation into Quiché of the Gospel of Mark and the Gospel of Luke into the Cachequel [*sic*], as to whether they have proved useful or not in evangelizing Indians.

Mr. Legters moved that it is the sense of this body that although present methods have reached a certain number of Indians,

29

that the Indians of Guatemala should have the Gospel of the Lord Jesus Christ in a written form in their own languages.

On motion of Mr. Dinwiddie, the meeting was adjourned for the night with prayer.

January 24th, 1921

The Chairman opened the meeting by asking for requests for prayer, and after receiving definite requests as to the personal needs of the members present, the meeting went to prayer.

The Chairman then announced that our first topic for consideration for the day is to discuss and decide upon methods for reaching Indians in their own languages.

Mr. Townsend asked Mr. Burgess if he could study the Indian language while living in Quezaltenango. Mr. Burgess replied that he finds it impossible to acquire the Indian tongue without living among the Indians and that men must be separated for this particular work.

Mr. Legters asked how this is to be accomplished. Mr. Burgess states that missionaries should be prayed out who will live and learn right with the Indians. Mr. Legters called attention to the fact that Peter and Paul got together to decide how the work was to be done and they decided that the whole business of Paul was with evangelizing the Gentiles and of Peter the Jews, and that we must well recognize the importance of rightly dividing the work between the workers.

Mr. Dinwiddie asked why Mr. Burgess and Mr. Townsend did not arrange during their anticipated stay of a couple of months among the Indians in their respective fields to translate the same Gospel and compare notes afterward.

Mr. Townsend suggested beginning with "Porciones Escogidas"; Mr. Robinson wants to begin with the Quiché translation of Mark; selecting all Cachequel [*sic*] words which occur in that work.

Mr. Burgess stated that it will be necessary to observe uniform rules by all who work on the translations.

On motion of Mr. Legters, it was resolved that Mr. Burgess and Mr. Townsend constitute themselves a Translating Committee, that they translate the Gospel separately and afterward come together to compare their translations. Unanimously carried.

Mr. Robinson then invited Messrs. Burgess and Townsend to Panajachel next September for this comparison.

The following remarks were then considered: That it is quite easy for Mr. Herbert Toms to learn an Indian language, having a perfect pronunciation of the Spanish. Mr. Frank Toms not able to manage their present large work alone.

Indians must be trained to do the work, but at least two missionaries should work with each tribe. Mr. Robinson touched 85,000 Cachiquels in his department; there are 150,000 Cachiquels in Mr. Townsend's district; there are 60,000 Cachiquels in Totonicapán; there are 60,000 Cachiquels in Quezaltenango.

There should be a missionary family for Totonicapán. There are over 300,000 Cachiquels in Guatemala.

In Quezaltenango there are also Mams, but there must be one special missionary given to them, so as not to mix up the different tribes.

Mr. Burgess stated that he cannot look to his Board to support Indian workers.

It was also stated that in Mexico there is one tribe which the Mexican Government makes no pretense of ever having conquered.

In Nicaragua the Moravian mission have 7000 Indian members of their churches.

The Indians of Del Norte need one missionary couple; the Mam tribe one couple; the Quichés two couples; the Cachiquels one couple; the Quechís one couple; the Cobáns two couples; and two single missionaries are needed for Townsend in the district of the Cachiquels. There are 200,000 Mams.

In order to begin the foundation work of giving the Gospel to the Indians in their different languages for the Republic of Guatemala, there are needed at the present time seven couples and two single women and two additional couples to relieve missionaries now occupied in Ladino work for Indian work. This was then made a motion, seconded, and unanimously passed.

On motion the meeting adjourned with prayer.

January 24th, 1921 (Evening session)

The conference reconvened after dinner, and after prayer the Chairman announced that the meeting had before it for consideration the Method of Organization, the auspices under which the new recruits for whom we are praying are to come to the field.

Mr. Burgess asked if there should be a separate organization for Indian work in Guatemala, known as The Latin American Indian Mission. Mr. Dinwiddie said he considered it a pity to have a separate organization if things can be arranged without it.

It was then discussed and decided that the Guatemalan Indian is our first problem; the next problem those of Mexico and lastly—the South American Indians, and that if God should give any of us a personal conviction of an interest beyond our present sphere of work we would join in carrying it out.

Mr. Burgess stated that we are not limited to our own immediate sphere but that our work is related to a much greater problem.

Mr. Dinwiddie stated that his conviction is that God is going to work for the Latin American Indian and that, in order to [do an] effective work, each one of us must have a vision of working and praying for the larger field. He also stated that there is in South America a little work in Ecuador, a little in Bolivia, and that in Paraguay there is a work which was intended for Indians but which became absorbed in Spanish work; also there is an existing work of the church of England between Paraguay and Bolivia.

Mr. Dinwiddie also stated that in going over the existing unevangelized fields and their possible source of supply from the denominations, he had found that there is only one pioneer work to be undertaken this year by them, and that is in Abyssinia.

The Chairman then called upon the meeting for personal expressions as to the character of any organization for the evangelization of the Latin Indians.

Mr. Townsend suggested an organization with a generous policy but giving the Indian first place.

Mr. Robinson said he would like to be in a prayer circle to pray for the Latin American Indians and to feel that there is one solid organization for the evangelization of all the Indians, with our native congregations contributing toward the larger work.

Mr. Toms thought an organization devoted to evangelizing all the Indians of Latin America would be of great help to local stations and deepen their zeal and spirit.

Mr. Legters stated that when God starts things he has great things in view.

Thereupon, on motion of Mr. Dinwiddie, it was resolved that it is the sense of this conference that in view of the fact that the problem of the unevangelized Indians is one and the same throughout Latin America, it would be desirable that a body be formed which, by contribution, by cooperation, by direct activity would evangelize the Indians of Latin America, reported to be over 40,000,000 in number. Unanimously carried.

This body would contribute to the direct organization, it would cooperate with others and engage in direct activity where the work was undone.

The members of this body who had knowledge of Indian work could be of immense value to new missionaries who wanted to go to pioneer fields.

Mr. Dinwiddie stated that no individual missionary can give all the necessary information; it is collective experience that will get the work done.

Mr. Townsend said it had been found that almost the only missionaries who have gone forth from Guatemala have been Indians. Chiquimula Mission have sent six Indian missionaries to Honduras. These Indian missionaries opened up the trail between Chiquimula and Tegucigalpa.

The matter of necessary Committees was discussed and it was suggested that the following committees be appointed:

1. A Committee to look after occupation of territory and cooperation with other missions, (If volunteers offered, they might become members of the missions already occupying the field) and to incite to greater activity the missions responsible for work already existing.

2. A Committee on Organization;

3. A Committee on Policy and Doctrine (The relation of the native brethren to this work shall be defined by the Committee on Policy).

4. A Committee on Women's and Children's Work.

It was moved and unanimously carried that the appointment of committees be left to the Chair.

Mr. Burgess then appointed the following committees:

Committee on Occupation and Cooperation: Mr. Burgess, Mr. Townsend, Mr. Toms.

Committee on Organization: Mr. Dinwiddie, Mr. Legters, Mr. Robinson, Mrs. Treichler.

Committee on Doctrine and Policy: Mr. Treichler, Mr. Legters, Mr. Toms.

Committee on Women's and Children's Work: Miss Williams, Mrs. Toms, Mrs. Burgess, Mrs. Townsend.

Adjourned with prayer.

January 25th, 1921

The conference reconvened at 3 p.m. and, after prayer, the Chairman called for the Report of the Committee on Occupation and Cooperation.

It was moved and unanimously received that no report should be acted upon until all reports should have been read.

Mr. Toms then read the report of the Committee on Occupation and Cooperation, as follows:

"In the matter of cooperation, the policy of this organization is to incite the various Mission Boards responsible for centers to undertake the adequate manning of the same. Wherever practicable, this organization will work through established agencies, seeking to aid them to procure recruits and funds for them. Where an established agency does not undertake the adequate reaching of the Indians, nor cares to do so, this organization will feel at liberty to occupy the field, if possible with the consent of the organization already occupying the territory.

"Since the object of this organization is to evangelize in the shortest possible time the Latin American Indians, it expresses its sincere willingness to cooperate with all sound, evangelical societies at work on the fields and expresses its willingness to turn over such work as it may have established when these organizations mentioned are equipped adequately to carry on the work along the lines laid down.

"As a matter of general principle, the unit of endeavor shall be tribal and this condition or consideration will determine the division of territory.

"Suggestions for the placing of the Indian workers:

For the Mam tribe: 1.   San Pedro Sacatepéquez
                        2.   San Ildefonso Ixtahuacán

For Del Norte tribe:	3.	San Miguel Acatán
For Cachiquel tribe:	4.	Quezaltenango for Quezaltenango, Such, and Retalileu [*sic*]
	5.	Totonicapán for Totonicapán and north of Quezaltenango
	6.	Panajachel for Sololá and part of Such
	7.	San Antonio for surrounding region
For Quiché tribe:	8.	Santo Tomás [Chichicastenango]
	9.	Zacualpa
For	10.	Near Cobán
	11.	Near Salamá."

Mr. Dinwiddie then read the draft of the report of the Committee on Organization, and stated that the prevailing idea is field direction.

"I. *Name.* The name of this association shall be _____
_____.

II. *Object.* The object of this association shall be, by contribution to and cooperation with other agencies and also by direct activity to give the Gospel to the Indians of Latin America.

III. *General Direction.* The management and direction of this association shall be vested in a General Council; the local government in a Field and Home Councils under the General Council.

IV. *Members of General Council.* The General Council shall be composed of all members of the Association both in Home and Field Councils.

V. *Members of Field Councils.* The members of the Field councils shall consist only of those 1) who believe they have been called of God to devote themselves primarily to the evangelization of the Indians of Latin America; 2) those who subscribe annually in writing to the doctrinal belief of the Association as their personal conviction; 3) those who have had experience in the winning of

35

souls and are actively engaged to that end; whose lives are surrendered to Christ as Lord and who reveal by the working of the Holy Spirit in them as examples to others the character of Christ in their service and everyday living; who work in hearty accord with the policies and practices of the Association as expressed by its General and Local Councils.

VI. *Members of Home Council.* The members of the Home Council shall be those only who believe that God has called them to give a contribution in prayer and service to the evangelization of the Indians of Latin America as one of the important parts of their service under Him; those who subscribe annually in writing to the doctrinal belief of the Association as part of their personal conviction; those who have had experience in the winning of souls and are actively engaged to that end; whose lives are surrendered to Christ as Lord and who reveal by the working of the Holy Spirit in them as examples to others the character of Christ in their service and everyday living; and who work in hearty accord with the policies and practices of the Association as expressed by its General and Local Councils.

VII. *Officers.*

[At this point we will skip several long paragraphs dealing with the general duties of Chairman, Secretary, and Treasurer of the General Council, the Field Council, and the Home Council.]

On motion of Mr. Legters, the draft of the report of the Committee on Organization was reread and considered section by section:

Name. It was unanimously resolved that the name of the Association should be The Latin American Indian Mission.

Object. It was unanimously resolved to approve the object of this Association as stated in the Organization Committee's report.

Membership. Mr. Burgess asked if it would be well to insert a clause relative to a language test. Discussion ruled this out. Mr. Robinson asked if provision should be made to exclude non-voting members from holding office, which point was not incorporated.

January 25, 1921 (evening session)

After a short season of prayer, Mr. Dinwiddie suggested that the officers of the General Council be identical with the officers of the Field Council for the time being, as Guatemala is the whole field at present.

On motion of Mr. Legters, it was resolved to pass upon the various Articles of the Rules of Organization one by one as read. . . . On motion of Mr. Townsend, the report of the Organization Committee was adopted as a basis of organization and beginning activity and Mr. Dinwiddie was appointed a Committee of one to go over it with the reports of the other committees and the opinions which we have expressed and submit to us later in fuller detail (especially as to By-laws, which have not been formed as yet) matters relating to operation. Unanimously carried.

Mr. Legters reported that the report on Policy had not been completed.

The report on Doctrinal Basis was then read, as follows:

"WE BELIEVE

1. In ONE GOD, revealed as existing in three equal persons: Father, Son and Holy Spirit.

2. In the full inspiration of the Old and New Testament.

3. In the virgin birth of the Lord Jesus Christ, His substitutionary suffering on the cross as the only means of salvation from sin and His bodily resurrection for our justification.

4. In the assurance of salvation through the finished work of Christ.

5. In salvation by faith without works, but good works as a manifestation of our faith.

6. We are united in the hope of the imminent bodily return of our Lord.

7. In the indwelling of the Spirit in every believer and filling for life and service to those who are yielded to Him.

8. In the will, power and the providence of God to meet our every need.

9. In the future state of unending blessedness for the saved with Christ and the state of unending conscious suffering for the lost.

10. In His present position as Head of the Church and the Lord and the Life of every believer.

11. That the primary responsibility of every believer is that of bringing men to accept Christ as their personal Savior."

37

On motion of Mr. Robinson the Doctrinal Policy was adopted after such modifications of a literary character should be made of the original draft as are necessary. Unanimously carried.

The report of the Committee on Occupation was then reread and on motion of Mr. Robinson was approved unanimously.

The report of the Committee on Work for Women and Children was then read, as follows:

"It is absolutely necessary for the missionary women engaged in Indian work to learn the Indian dialect. Bible classes or any special work for the women cannot be commenced until the missionary can speak their language. It is very seldom that an Indian woman understands the Spanish language.

Where possible the wife should accompany her husband on evangelization trips. It serves in bringing the women together and also they lose the false idea that it is a religion for men only.

Indian Bible women are needed. They can in their own tongue do a great work in the house-to-house visitation, and can be used of God in bringing the women to the Lord in a way that would be impossible for a foreigner.

The missionary's heart should be filled with a very special love, and be ready to help these poor ignorant women in things concerning themselves and their homes. Especially should they be willing to teach them how to care for their children. Mrs. Toms spoke of a series of letters on how to care for babies, written by a missionary in China. These should be translated into the Indian dialect and given to mothers.

THE CHILDREN: Schools should be conducted by native teachers. The children should have the first hour each morning in Bible study, to be conducted in the Indian tongue, copies of the Scriptures being in the hands of each child. Thus they are taught to read the Scriptures in their own tongue, so that in their homes they may be able to give the Word of God to the entire family, acquainting them with the Scriptures in their native tongue. This will also prevent the children from forgetting the dialect even when learning the Spanish language. The children should not be permitted to use the dialect during school hours outside of this Bible study class.

An American teacher should be located in a Mission Center. She should occupy herself in training more advanced pupils as teachers. She should superintend schools in her district and should every three months visit one of the schools in her district, having all teachers from other towns meet with her in that particular place for conference with the teachers as well as to inform as to actual conditions in the school. Of course for each conference with the teachers she should meet with them in the different schools in the district. This would mean an advance in the schools in the district, as well as be a great blessing to the teachers having this personal touch with the missionary.

Wherever Sunday Schools are opened, classes for the children should be organized."

Whereupon, the foregoing report was on motion of Mr. Robinson, adopted as read.

The Chairman then announced that the status of the Mission as to its working on a faith basis or not, should be discussed, and also whether the workers will be guaranteed their support or whether the Council will uphold the worker in prayer for his support.

On motion of Mr. Legters, it was resolved that a Committee of two be appointed (of which Mr. Dinwiddie should be one) to prepare a policy for a financial basis of the Mission, which shall be incorporated with the report on Organization, and be submitted to the Mission when Mr. Dinwiddie has prepared it. Mr. Dinwiddie then asked Mrs. Burgess to serve with him on this Committee, and they retired from the meeting to prepare this policy.

On motion of Mr. Townsend, it was decided to proceed with the organization of the Field Council, which shall function as a General Council to begin activities at home.

The meeting then proceeded to the election of officers.

On motion of Mr. Townsend, it was resolved to vote by ballot and the persons receiving the two highest number of ballots to receive the nomination.

Thereupon a ballot was cast for Chairman resulting in a tie between Mr. Burgess and Mr. Townsend; a second ballot was taken showing a majority in favor of Mr. Burgess, which on motion was made unanimous.

A ballot was then taken for secretary, resulting in a majority for Mrs. Treichler, which was also on motion made a unanimous vote.

The balloting for Treasurer was then done, Mr. Robinson receiving the majority of votes, which on motion was made unanimous.

The meeting then proceeded to elect officers for the General Council.

Mr. Robinson then nominated Mr. Dinwiddie as General Director of the Latin American Indian Mission, and he was unanimously elected.

Mr. Dinwiddie then reentered the meeting and the Chairman announced to Mr. Dinwiddie our earnest desire that he accept under God our call as General Director. Mr. Dinwiddie then expressed his entire willingness to do anything in his power for this Mission but requested time to pray with Mrs. Dinwiddie about the matter and to let us know later.

On motion of Mr. Townsend, the meeting then resolved to ask Mr. Dinwiddie to act as Executive Secretary for the Home Council pending his acceptance of the General Directorship. Unanimously carried.

On motion of Mr. Townsend, it was resolved that the Chairman constitute a committee of one to report on a publication to be issued in the States by this Mission, which was unanimously carried with the amendment to including Mr. Dinwiddie on the Committee, and suggesting the name "The Latin American Indian."

On motion of Mr. Townsend, Mr. Legters was asked to serve on the Home Council. Unanimously carried.

The meeting adjourned at twelve o'clock midnight after prayer. HALLELUJAH! "IT IS TIME FOR JEHOVAH TO WORK."

L. H. Treichler,

Secretary(15)

The financial policy drawn up by Mr. Dinwiddie and Mrs. Burgess reads as follows:

The financial basis of the Mission shall be to depend utterly upon the infallible faithfulness of God to provide for the needs of His servants in the work to which He has called them. The responsibility of the Officers and Members of the Councils shall be to keep informed as to the sufficiency of funds in the Treasury and to be faithful in prayer, life, service and personal giving for the needs of the workers.

There shall be no guarantee of funds beyond what is in the treasury and no debts incurred. (The Executive Secretaries and the General Director shall be on the same financial basis as the missionaries.)(16)

Correspondence from this period reveals some of the discussion that went on in regard to finances. A letter from Dinwiddie to Townsend states that "Toms and Mr. Burgess were of one mind that the support of the Indian workers could be secured from the Indians" themselves, and that the eventual goal would be indigenous tribal churches, even though initial support for Indian evangelists would be secured from the United States.(17)

The Chichicastenango Twelve fully expected to recruit new missionaries who would go out under the L.A.I.M. rather than under the older agencies. Townsend suggested "That members of established missions should be 'associate members' of the L.A.I.M." and that the L.A.I.M. should be responsible for the financial support of its active members and give the surplus to its associate members.(18)

As one can see from reading the foregoing minutes, one of the main goals of the L.A.I.M. was Bible translation. Burgess informed his board that Townsend, Robinson and he had been named a committee of three to translate the New Testament into Cakchiquel.

Townsend had already learned a great deal about that language and had begun to translate Mark's Gospel. But he wanted the input of other translators. Later Townsend and Burgess did occasionally meet for a week at a time to go over the translation together, but not as often as Townsend would have liked. He wrote a year after the Chichicastenango Conference: "I wish that Burgess were nearer to consult on translation work but as he isn't, I must go with what advice Robinson and the native workers can give me."(19)

Another goal of the L.A.I.M. was to survey the Indian fields and assess the needs, with a view to getting recruits, finances, and prayer support for the unreached tribes. "The missionaries insisted that the greatest need was a thorough study of the Indian problem of the republic as a whole, as the information in hand was only too fragmentary," observed an article in *The Sunday School Times* which reported on Dinwiddie's visit to Guatemala and the Chichicastenango Conference.(20)

Legters, in particular, was most eager to study "the distribution, numbers, characteristics and strategic centers" of the various tribes. Following the Chichicastenango Conference, he spent three months surveying seven Guatemalan tribes, and returned to various parts of Latin America year after year to conduct similar surveys.

While in Chichicastenango, Dinwiddie and Legters not only launched the L.A.I.M., but they also held special meetings for the national workers who were present. These Victorious Life messages were "singularly blessed."

A young Hispanic woman named Elvira Ruiz, who already knew some Quiché as a result of trading with the Indians, dedicated her life to missionary service in the Dinwiddie meetings. Later she became a missionary under the Primitive Methodist Board.

Many of the Quiché and Cakchiquel leaders who attended the meetings made similar spiritual commitments, and Paul Burgess reported the following about the "awakening" which broke out at the conference:

> One of the most remarkable aspects of this new awakening has been a wave of evangelistic zeal which has lifted the Indians who were already believers out of the routine of ordinary church life, and has made their churches centers from which scores of evangelists are going out to evangelize their fellow-countrymen.(21)

The meetings were a spiritual "high" for all concerned. Dinwiddie, however, warned the missionaries that testings were bound to come, both to the organization and to its individual members; and Legters even went so far as to suggest that due to the opposition which was to be expected, the "associate members" of the L.A.I.M. might have to resign from their respective mission boards and become "active members" of the new agency. Burgess evidently considered this possibility, for he wrote to Walker Eugene McBath (who had pioneered among the Quichés from 1903 to 1913 and was still deeply interested in them):

> There has been a new organization formed to work for the Indians which is still in the formative period. We are connected with it but do not know yet whether it will mean our severing relations with the Board.(22)

When the Chichicastenango Conference was over, the missionaries returned to their respective stations full of enthusiasm. Louise Treichler's letter to the Home Council of the Central American Mission is representative of the "great inspiration and blessing" which the twelve had received:

> On January 23rd, we had with us a large number of the missionaries who are devoting their time to the Indian work. Also, there were more than thirty Indian workers and believers from the territories of Mr. Burgess, Mr. Townsend, and ourselves. We had a great time providing for sleeping and feeding so many, but it was indeed a happy privilege and the Lord provided all we needed . . . We also had with us Messrs. Dinwiddie and Legters, whose visit has been a great inspiration and blessing to us all. The aim of the conference was to accomplish the evangelization of the Latin American Indians in this generation, and to do this, it is necessary to reach them in their own tongues, the number of which is legion.(23)

Two things may be noted in this quote. In the first place, the influence of the Student Volunteer Movement is strongly felt in the phrase, "The aim of the conference was to accomplish the evangelizaton of the Latin American Indians in this generation."

Secondly, it is interesting to note that Mrs. Treichler did not mention that a new organization had been spawned. Perhaps she was concerned, even then, that the home office of her mission would consider a new organization to be a threat. Perhaps she already sensed that testings would come, just as Rev. Dinwiddie had predicted.

3

THE VISION IS TESTED

A. BLESSING

Dinwiddie and Legters were sure that God had set His seal upon the new-born L.A.I.M. Shortly after completing his first survey trip, Legters wrote to Paul Burgess:

> I am sending to Mr. Robinson a draft for $300 for the Santa María station as per my promise. It came from the first person I talked with after reaching the states. I barely mentioned the place, in fact I have forgotten what I said, and here it is .... I am so glad that I can send you this money, the first I have gotten since reaching the states. I am as sure that for all the other needs He will send the men and the money.(24)

Burgess replied that half the money would be used for the first year's salary for Trinidad Aguilar, an evangelist who was assigned to Santa María. He added, "We shall use the surplus to either rent or build a shelter where those who continually pass through Santa María can spend the night and hear the Gospel."(25)

Dinwiddie was just as enthusiastic as Legters about the initial response of Christians in the United States. Only two months after the Chichicastenango Conference, he reported that support from the U.S.A. had been pledged for seven national workers, and that two full-time missionary candidates were in sight.(26)

Within six months, the number of pledges and of possible candidates had more than doubled. Dinwiddie wrote to Townsend:

> You will, I know, share the deep gratitude Mr. Legters and I are feeling because of the seal God has set upon the L.A.I.M. There has been received by us, without any solicitation, and forwarded to the field, the first installments of the pledges for the support of seventeen native workers and we have in hand the names of seventeen possible candidates who desire to go to work among the Indians of Guatemala.(27)

Furthermore, reports from the field were encouraging. Dinwiddie wrote to Townsend expressing his views on the importance of Bible translation:

> I rejoice especially in the translation of the book of Mark into the lingua—not that this work is the only work needed but that it has been so long neglected and seems to be the most important of all.(28)

Townsend was not only translating the New Testament; he had also initiated a Bible training school for Cakchiquel evangelists. Burgess, although not yet free for exclusively Indian work, was also doing Bible translation. In addition, he was sending out Quiché-speaking Bible salesmen, some of them supported through the fund-raising efforts of Dinwiddie and Legters, and others through the profits from Burgess' own bookstore. These men were going into such remote and hostile Quiché centers as the city of Nagualá. Two Mam evangelists in the department of Huehuetenango were being supported through the gifts which Robinson, as field treasurer, transmitted to Herbert Toms. God had, indeed, set His seal upon the budding effort.

B. TESTING

Nevertheless, along with the blessing, there was severe testing, just as Dinwiddie had predicted at Chichicastenango. Criticism, misunderstanding, and illness seemed to plague each of the Chichicastenango Twelve. And the boards under which they were working did not at first seem sympathetic to the new venture.

1. Presbyterian Reaction

Burgess wrote to his board in glowing terms about the new organization, although without referring to the L.A.I.M. by name.

Stanley White, the board's secretary, responded with not a little uneasiness:

> I am intensely interested in what you say about the Indian work and should like to have further information on the following points: First, in the conference on January 22nd was it composed of representatives of the various missions or of individuals who are interested in Indian work? Who are the Rev. Howard Dinwiddie and the Rev. Leonard Legters? I am not familiar with the inside workings of the Victorious Life Testimony Committee, but our experience with men who lay stress upon the Victorious Life testimony has been in times past a very unsatisfactory one. Are they people who are laying particular stress upon the pre-millenium views?
>
> . . . Another point that I would like to know about would be where you say a committee of three was named to begin work, one of them being yourself. What is meant by your having drawn up the constitution of a Mission which is to work in heartiest cooperation with all evangelical agencies already at work in this field, and which is to ask for recruits and funds apart from established agencies? I fear that here also you may be treading upon dangerous ground. The course that I would advise would be that you lay this work upon the hands of regular representatives of the regular mission work and cooperate with them rather than to organize a new mission of an independent character. . . .
>
> What do you mean also when you say that we mapped out the Republic by Indian tribes and laid responsibility upon the Boards now operating in the territories in question? Does that mean any

different status from that which now exists? I had assumed that our mission particularly in connection with Quezaltenango was attempting at least to carry this responsibility now.

I should hope, my dear Mr. Burgess, that in regard to this Indian work you would discuss the whole matter thoroughly in the mission and then send word to the Board with all the emphasis you can what you feel to be the Board's responsibility and then let us see what we can do. Naturally I cannot promise what the Board's reaction will be but I personally am so much interested in pushing this work among Indians that I shall be entirely in sympathy with making a very determined effort to enlarge our field in this direction. (29)

Burgess' answer to Stanley White was frank:

Now in regard to the Indian work I will take up your questions in the order in which they are asked. The conference held last January was not attended by any of us as official representatives of the Missions with which we are identified but rather as individuals who are interested in Indian work.

The Rev. Howard Dinwiddie is a scion of an old Virginia family. I think his father was a Presbyterian minister and he is a Baptist if I mistake not. A brother is President of Tulane University in New Orleans. Rev. Dinwiddie was an inspector of Public Institutions in New York during the administration of Mitchell and I understand had quite a part in the fight of the latter against the catholic hierarchy. I judge that he is not a premillenialist. At least he has several times withstood in a tactful way the extreme premillenialist views of some of the missionaries here on the field. The Rev. Leonard Legters was ordained in the Dutch Reformed Church, was many years a missionary to the Indians of Oklahoma and California and has for the past ten years been connected with the Southern Presbyterian Church as pastor at Bishopville, S. C.

As to undertaking work in connection with those who hold premillenarian views in extreme forms we are not likely to run up against any worse cases of this than we already have to deal with here on the field. But even the most eccentric premillenarian is infinitely far ahead of the Indian witch doctor who offers human sacrifices. Personally I think the premillenarian view more in accord with the teaching of Scripture than the post-millenarian view, though of course I believe in making our plans for an indefinitely long future of Christian life on this planet. But as I say it does not

47

appear to be likely that we are going to have any friction in this regard as we have managed to get along harmoniously with some very extreme premillenarians in this field.

As to the organizing of a new mission body which while cooperating with existing organizations might secure money and recruits independently, I see your point and realize the dangers entailed in launching too many organizations. But if existing organizations rise to the opportunity before them, the new body will be superfluous as a money raising and recruiting agency and be simply a conference for the exchange of views and experiences and the formulating of policies in Indian work. If the existing agencies do not take up the work of Indian evangelization it seems that the Indian should not be compelled to wait for the Gospel if there is a way of getting it to him. . . .

Now in regard to the mapping out of the Republic by Indian tribes and the laying of responsibility upon the Boards now cooperating in the territories in question this may mean a very similar arrangement to the present or a very different one. If the existing Boards will send missionaries to take up Indian work in their respective fields, all will continue as at present. If they do not, this new mission would feel justified in entering a given territory assigned to a Mission which was doing only Spanish work where Indian work was required. As you say our Mission is *attempting* to carry this responsibility in the Quezaltenango field now. The way it is *doing* so is to put one lone missionary in charge of about 70 Spanish-speaking congregations and 9 schools among the Spanish-speaking people and 6 Spanish-speaking evangelists and then tell him that what time he has left over he can give to the Indians and to appropriate $1,350 for this Spanish-speaking work and not one cent for the Indian work. If in addition to the Spanish work we now have 12 Indian congregations and 2 Indian evangelists this is due not to our Mission but to the Indians themselves who have come by themselves and who are supporting their own evangelists. [The two evangelists referred to are Marcelino Vásquez, who supported himself, and Pedro Poz, who was supported by local believers.]

Yet the Indians make up fully 3/4 of the inhabitants of the Department [province] and a way must be found to take them the Gospel in their own tongue. The new workers who have come into the Lake of Atitlán district are Cameron Townsend and wife, a Presbyterian who passed his Junior year in Occidental College and is located under the Central American Mission at San Antonio Aguas Calientes, and Rev. Robinson and wife at Panajachel. Mr. Robinson was graduated from Occidental College last year and ordained by the Baptists and Mr. and Mrs. Treichler who have taken over the work of Dr. Secord at Chichicastenango. Mr. Townsend, Mr. Robinson and I are the committee on language to do the preliminary work toward a translation of the Bible into Catshiquel [*sic*].

As you suggest the mission take action in the matter we will seek to do so within a few days. I think if you will examine the minutes of our past meetings you will see that we have several times taken action in recent years but the Board has never been able to do anything to realize the projects we have formed. Now this new opportunity presents itself. If the Sullenbergers can return to the field this will help us very much indeed, as it will mean that Mrs. Burgess and myself can be freed to learn the Indian languages and to do Indian work.(30)

White's answer shows that Burgess' letter had "sunk deeply" into his heart. How feeble, indeed, had been the Presbyterian efforts to reach the vast Indian population of Guatemala! He added:

The one thing that I am concerned with is that you should not be withheld for any proper service to the Indian work, and I hope that the Mission, with you, will devise some way by which this can be done.(31)

The vision that was born in Chichicastenango thus spread to New York, to the headquarters of the Presbyterian Board. Within a few months, Rev. and Mrs. Linn Sullenberger were in Quezaltenango to take over the Spanish work, and the Burgesses were free to concentrate on Quiché language study and translation.

2. C.A.M. Reaction

If the Presbyterian Board was cautious and even suspicious about the new mission, the leaders of the Central American Mission were even more vigorously opposed.

A. Edward Bishop, an early C.A.M. missionary, stands tall in its annals as a bold pioneer and church planter. Nevertheless, as early as 1907 he opposed the use of Indian languages.

When he heard about the new organization formed in Chichicastenango, he drew up a list of seven criticisms. These were presented in writing to Cameron Townsend. What place was there for a new mission which would compete with established work, distribute funds through unauthorized channels, go against the time-honored policy of assimilating Indians into the Spanish-speaking churches, and encourage association with individuals who were *not* premillenialists?

Although the list of seven criticisms is not now available, one can imagine Bishop's strong language.

Bishop had previously written a letter to Burgess criticizing him for attending an inter-church conference in Guatemala City. This conference was attended by Baptists, Presbyterians, Methodists, and independents such as Harry Strachan of Costa Rica. Among other items on its agenda was the establishment of Indian schools in Guatemala. But Bishop wrote:

> In the face of the fact that the major part of the apostasy of Protestantism is linked up with the Inter-Church-World Movement, if we give the advice to the Christian of Central America that you propose—how can we be free from their blood? If the bugle give an uncertain sound how can the Lord's immature sheep be warned against the huge wolf of apostasy?

The letter continues with fervent admonitions to "come out from among them and be separate" and to have nothing to do with inter-church cooperation upon which rests "the anathema of God."(32)

The above letter is quoted merely to show Bishop's zeal for orthodoxy and also to show the kind of strong language he was capable of using. We may thus imagine that his seven-fold criticism of the L.A.I.M. was equally forceful in its language.

Another problem which surfaced shortly after Legters returned to the United States was that, in his zeal for gaining new recruits for Indian work, he stated in Washington, D. C., that "in fact no one was doing work among the Indians except Mr. Burgess and Mr. Townsend."

In the audience sat Anne Alloway McBath. She had gone

to Guatemala as a single missionary under the Central American Mission. There she met Presbyterian Walker Eugene McBath, married him, and joined his board in 1906. The couple worked among the Quiché Indians for several years prior to the arrival of the Burgesses, and the first Quiché converts were fruits of their ministry. In 1911 they buried their only son in Quezaltenango. They mourned him not only because of parental love, but also because his winsome ways had begun to give them an entrance into the hearts of the Quiché people. And they told their supporters that, in spite of their grief, they were more determined than ever to start a Bible and agricultural school for the Quichés. In 1913 they resigned from the Presbyterian board and opened an independent work in the city of Almolonga, where they succeeded in teaching the Quiché Indians of that region to grow a variety of vegetables— not just corn. Economic problems, however, forced them to leave the field before their vision for a Bible and agricultural school had been fulfilled.

As she listened to Legters, Anne McBath was deeply hurt. Hadn't the Jacob Cassels raised up a whole Indian congregation in San Marcos without using the Mam language? Was not Herbert Toms endeavoring to reach the Mams of Huehuetenango, even though he preached entirely in Spanish? Mr. Bishop had certainly been used of God to raise up congregations among the Cakchiquel Indians even before Townsend appeared on the field! And what about the Quiché people whom she and her husband had sought to evangelize and teach? Mrs. McBath wrote: "I feel that there is a lack of the Spirit of God in this new movement—that there is no recognition of the judgment of the council of the older missionaries, and that what they have already done among the Indians doesn't count."(33) And her letter came into the hands of Mr. Bishop.

Bishop was already upset by the L.A.I.M. and by a *Sunday School Times* article which suggested that Townsend and Burgess were the only two missionaries who were reaching the Indians of Guatemala. Anne McBath's letter upset him further.

51

He wrote to Dinwiddie:

> I am asking the Lord that both you and Mr. Borton may see the need of exercising very special care in the selection of the men whom the Victorious Life Testimony are to send to Central America this fall....
> When I read Bro. Legters' article on Central America in the *Sunday School Times,* I sought to find whereby I could justify his blunders. It did not occur to me that they would be repeated. When these blunders and others of a similar nature become the basis of a wide and permanent propaganda as indicated by the Washington, D. C., event, then you will understand how keenly we feel their danger.
> . . .
> The Indian problem because of its magnitude and partial neglect demands definite, concentrated action. My vision and that of Mr. Townsend speaks of cooperation but not of separation. Repeatedly you have told me that sound existing agencies would be recognized, strengthened, and cooperated with. This is as it should be, and by the grace of God is what I am confident will yet be carried out. To separate the Indian work from the Spanish, at least in the territory in which Mr. Townsend and myself are working, would be like picking woof and warp apart. Such action would be deplorable and would bring no end of dissatisfaction as well as damage to the whole work.
> I think it would please the Lord for you and Mr. Borton and Mr. Trumbull to take unto yourselves dear Bro. Legters and expound unto him a better way, a method more sane and a broader view point.(34)

Townsend, with the inborn diplomatic ability which characterized him all his life, tried to smooth things over. He wrote Dinwiddie that Mr. Bishop's forceful criticism "has given me only a strong desire that our organization be perfected and the objections which he has raised may be overcome in such a way as to win the confidence of him and all concerned."(35)

In another letter he stated: "If we really live up to the high ideals set forth in the constitution we drew up at Chichicastenango, we will live down all just attacks and we don't need to mind about the unjust."(36)

With Townsend's tactful words, Bishop began to worry less about the L.A.I.M., but the Home Council of the Central American Mission continued to be suspicious. Dinwiddie tried to meet with the council members, but was put off time after time. He complained to Townsend about the "unexplainable inability of Dr. Pettingill and Mr. Smith" (both on the C.A.M. Board) to meet and discuss the Indian problem. (This was the same Mr. Smith who later was so vigorously opposed to Townsend's translation efforts.)

Luther Rees, on the other hand, was willing to talk to Legters and Dinwiddie. Rees was one of the three original laymen who had prayed with Dr. Scofield for the evangelization of Central America. In 1890, when the C.A.M. was founded, he became the first president of its home council, a position which he held for fifty years.

Rees was known as an intercessor and as a man of wisdom and seasoned experience. Although he was happy for Legters and Dinwiddie to cooperate with the C.A.M. in Indian work, he felt that the L.A.I.M. was a superfluous agency.

He wrote to Dinwiddie:

> The C.A. Mission Council met at the Moody Institute, July 15 to 17. We were very sorry that you could not be with us, but we took it all from Him.
>
> A resolution was passed expressing our appreciation of your visit to Central America and of your deep interest in the work among the Indians. The Council felt that while it did not seem necessary that another society should now be organized to carry on the work among the Indians of Central America, it would heartily welcome the cooperation of Brother Legters and yourself in the work of evangelizing these Aborigines so long neglected.
>
> The members of the Council still hope for the opportunity to go into this matter with you both more fully, and that soon. We should like very much to come to an understanding as to how funds for this work should be administered,—whether they should be sent directly to the Missionaries or through Judge Scott our Treasurer, who has the whole work in his mind as well as on his heart. We feel that it

will avoid confusion if the latter plan is adopted. We always forward special funds promptly.

We think you can see that if one of our Missionaries is working under two boards, the results may not be the best. We would not object to his administering funds sent for native workers or for special purposes consistent with the principles of the Mission, but if these funds passed through our hands we would know just what he was doing. The next best plan, in case you feel you must send funds to the Missionaries of the C.A.M. would be for you to send to Judge Scott a memorandum of these remittances so that we would have all the facts in hand.

As to applicants for Missionary appointment, we would want to pass upon them in the regular way. We have found that great care should be exercised in sending out workers under the plan adopted by this Mission. The applicant as well as the Council must be sure the Lord is leading. Quite a large proportion of the applicants never go out. It is much better to do this sifting at home, rather than on the field.(37)

At least one good thing came from all the misunderstandings on the part of the Presbyterian and C.A.M. boards. Both agencies began to be more aware than ever before of the Indians and their needs, and both began to do more to meet those needs. Dinwiddie recognized this and wrote:

In spite of misunderstandings, it seems apparent that a great stimulus has been given to the Indian work not only in creating interest and contributions, but also in the reaction of the conference at Chichicastenango and consequent results upon the boards.(38)

In the years to follow, both the Presbyterians and the C.A.M. began to send out more and more missionaries specifically assigned to Indian work and to Bible translation. These efforts will be dealt with more fully in later chapters.

3. Reaction of Other Boards

In addition to his futile attempts to meet with the C.A.M. council members, Dinwiddie tried to talk to denominational leaders in the U.S.A., for he wanted the L.A.I.M. to be a cooperative venture in every way. Dr. Thomas Moffett, Secretary of Indian Work for the Presbyterian Board of Home Missions, was cordial and enthusiastic about the new organization. The Moravians, on the other hand, had reservations about such a large-scale work among Indian peoples.

Since they had pioneered in evangelism and Bible translation among the Miskito Indians, Dinwiddie hoped that the Moravians would also be interested in other tribes. But the Moravian leaders felt that the L.A.I.M. should "seek to enable those now on the field to do thorough work, rather than to begin new missions, which could not be adequately worked."(39) They were obviously not interested in expansion.

4. Personal Testing of Individuals

The Treichlers. Following their mountain-top experience at the conference which they hosted, the Treichlers went through some deep valleys of testing. The Chichicastenango Twelve had agreed to meet a year later for a second L.A.I.M. conference. But Louise Treichler wrote to Paul Burgess that they would be unable to host the second conference and that she was resigning as secretary. "I am as yet unable to do the writing of my part of the minutes but will submit them later to Mrs. Burgess," she informed him.(40)

Furthermore, the Treichlers were discouraged about not receiving funds for a full-time Indian worker for their field. Dinwiddie's deputation efforts in the U.S.A. had resulted in a pledge for "the Treichler worker" and the money was coming in month after month, but it accumulated in the homeland, unused. Finally, when Dinwiddie became convinced that the Treichlers were unlikely to find a worker, he arranged for the funds to be transferred to one of the Quiché workers in the Burgess field, lest the donor become discouraged and stop giving.

Cameron Townsend reacted to this news with dismay, and conveyed his concern to Burgess:

> I have been told that the Treichlers have in some way or other been eliminated. Was that by action of our local committee or of

the executive officers? A letter just received from Mr. Dinwiddie makes me think that he is unaware of the fact that the Treichlers are doing Indian work to any extent at all. Now I don't know just how much they are doing but I do know that part of last year they had two Indian workers with them and hundreds of Indians have heard the gospel in their own tongue. I haven't had a chance to see the Treichlers yet since my return so that I haven't direct information from them but I think that they still have the Indians very much at heart . . . I hardly think that I can continue to serve on the committee if the Treichlers are not made one of us.(41)

In spite of Townsend's loyalty to the Treichlers and his desire to see them continue in Indian work, they dropped out of the Indian picture almost completely within a year of the Chichicastenango Conference. By 1924, they had resigned from the C.A.M. due to Mrs. Treichler's "nervous condition" and a doctrinal controversy over baptism. Although later reinstated as missionaries for a brief time, their enthusiasm never again soared to the heights it had reached in 1921.

What caused them to become drop-outs? Perhaps they were bothered by Mr. Bishop's seven criticisms of the L.A.I.M. Their lack of language ability could also have hindered their progress in Indian work. Perhaps the nervous strain of so much entertaining and traveling was more than Louise Treichler could bear. A retired missionary who knew both Louise Treichler and Elvira Townsend states that both had similar emotional problems. And the Burgesses felt that the disparity in age and education between Ben and Louise caused a strain on their marriage and ministry.

The problems faced by Louise Treichler were common to missionary wives in those days. Of the five women who attended the Chichicastenango Conference in 1921, three suffered a nervous breakdown at one time or another: Louise Treichler, Elvira Townsend, and Dora Burgess. (Dora had already recovered two years before the conference.)

Living conditions were primitive, medical help was remote, and linguistic work was extremely difficult. There was no S.I.L. to help young missionaries learn how to decode an unwritten language. As a result, language learning itself was very frustrating. Small wonder that many missionaries became discouraged or ill!

The Townsends. Illness was one of the chief trials which the Townsends faced after the Chichicastenango Conference. Elvira's emotional problems became so acute that she left for medical treatment in the United States only a few months after that gathering. Cameron followed her that fall, leaving his newly formed Bible training school, with nearly twenty students, in the hands of Robinson and a Cakchiquel teacher named Brígido. While in the U.S.A., he visited supporting churches and did not immediately return to Guatemala. Consequently, he was not at the second L.A.I.M. field conference, and his absence was another severe test, as will be seen in a later chapter.

The Burgesses. Paul Burgess, too, was constantly troubled by illness. Tropical fevers, inadequate meals, and nights spent on the road in tick-infested lowlands and wind-blown highlands were all taking their toll. He battled a persistent cough and sinus infection, his body ached, and his hands and feet felt either numb or prickly, as though swarms of insects were crawling up and down them.

Ella Williams. Miss Williams was also tested, although not by illness. Just after the Chichicastenango Conference, an ebullient A. B. Treichler wrote to Burgess: "Expecting much for our own lives and ministry in the new association and effort for the Indians . . . We're so glad Miss Williams could be one of us and we hope she will stay in Indian work."(42)

But Ella Williams was unable to fulfill her dream of starting a school for Quiché Indians. She was desperately needed at the *La Patria* School in Quezaltenango for a time, and in 1924 she was transferred to the Guatemala City *La Patria* because of a personnel shortage there. Later, she was needed at home to care for aging parents in their final years. (It was only later in life that she was able to return to Guatemala as the second wife of pioneer missionary Edward Haymaker.)

Legters, too, had his problems. He had a seriously ill wife to care for, and besides, it seemed to him that he had a knack for being misunderstood by the leaders of the C.A.M. Why did they take so many of his statements the wrong way?

Dinwiddie was not without personal difficulties and pressures, either. He was overworked and involved in too many organizations in the United States. His sensitive spirit felt keenly the misunderstandings that continued to arise with the C.A.M. leaders and even with his dear friend Cameron Townsend, who wanted him to join the Cakchiquel work rather than to stay in the U.S.A. to recruit new missionaries.

Dinwiddie's warning that trials were bound to come had surely come true. Yet, the majority of the Chichicastenango Twelve were determined to go on in spite of the setbacks. The vision which was born in January 1921 should not be allowed to wither and die, but should rather be broadened and expanded. The unevangelized ethnic groups of Latin America *must* be reached, in their own language, "in this generation."

4

THE VISION SPREADS TO PHILADELPHIA

A. THE INDIAN MISSION COMMITTEE OF AMERICA

Back in Philadelphia, Rev. Dinwiddie was actively engaged in seeking to incorporate the L.A.I.M. The organization had a field council, elected in Chichicastenango. But a home council was needed before the agency could be officially incorporated. Dinwiddie consulted with his friends at the Victorious Life Testimony, and also with Dr. Thomas Moffett of the Presbyterian Board of Home Missions, and then sent out a plea for prayer and an invitation to meet at a "Conference on the Latin American Indians."

I quote large portions of this circular letter to show the scope of Dinwiddie's vision and concern:

Philadelphia, Pennsylvania
August 12, 1921

Dear Friend:

The neglected Indian populations to the South of us in this Western Hemisphere have been a burden of responsibility, concern and prayer upon the hearts of a number of Christian men and women. Almost nineteen hundred years have passed since our Lord Jesus gave His life on Calvary's cross, purchased salvation for men, brought life and immortality to light in the Gospel, and gave to His disciples the great commission to disciple all the nations, teaching them to observe whatsoever He had commanded. And from the whole world today the millions of the native American race in Mex-

59

of unevangelized and untaught people, in proportion to their total number, of any element of earth's inhabitants. Here are whole lands and nations, tribes and communities, predominantly Indian in race, almost untouched by Christian agencies, living and dying "without God and without hope in the world."

In Ecuador 870,000 are Indians out of a population of 1,250,000. In Peru 57 per cent of the population is Indian; in Bolivia 50.9 per cent; in Guatemala 70 per cent. In Brazil the estimate is as high as seven to eight million Indians and the names of 373 tribes are reported in the Amazon valley. "Eighty per cent of the Central Americans cannot read a line of print" is the report of one of the greatest world travelers. . . .

Dinwiddie then went on to quote Frederick Palmer, an authority on Central America:

"People a day's sail from the United States degenerate for want of opportunities for education and religious training, while our missionaries spread light in darkest Africa and the interior of China. *This is the most backward region outside of Central Asia. . . .*"

Further on, Dinwiddie quoted Robert Speer's observations after his six months' tour of South America:

"The most needy and uncared for sections are the Indians of the Amazon, the Aymaras of Bolivia, the Quichuas of Bolivia and Peru, and the tribes of Ecuador and Colombia. There are savages among these Indians, but they are not inaccessible. . . ."

Dinwiddie then issued a call to prayer and action:

IMPRESSED WITH THIS VAST NEED; IMPELLED BY THE SPIRIT OF GOD, AS WE HUMBLY TRUST, AND PERSUADED THAT THE GOSPEL IS THE POWER OF GOD UNTO SALVATION, WE WHO NOW ADDRESS YOU ISSUE A CALL FOR A CONFERENCE ON THE LATIN AMERICAN INDIANS AT PHILADELPHIA IN THE FRIENDS ARCH STREET CENTER, 304 ARCH STREET, ON TUESDAY AND WEDNESDAY, SEPTEMBER 13TH AND 14TH, 1921 . . . .

From 2:30 to 3 o'clock (daylight saving time) on Tuesday afternoon the conference will engage in intercession. We ask that those absent compute the corresponding time wherever they may be in this land or other lands, and together we will seek in intercession to know God's will and leading. You are also asked to write one of the signers of this letter, sending your desires for the conference, and the addresses of any friends who are sharing in this burden and hope, to whom you would like this invitation mailed.

Let us pray: —That volunteers may be led to offer for this service. That we may "know what spirit we are of" as servants of the Master, and may seek that in all things He may have the pre-eminence.

That the right leaders, who can be most used of God may be indicated . . . .

The following considerations are to be in mind for discussion:

1. "The continent of neglect" and "The continent of opportunity." The Indians, the most needy and most overlooked people in the world.

2. Native converts evangelizing their race and tribes in their own language. Every recruit for the Church a recruiter.

3. Evangelism and Faith in God's Word and God's Power. No other Name and no other Power. A witness and testimony that the divine remedy for the needs of sinful men is all-sufficient.

4. A pioneer work. The Indian field singled out as a racial problem, requiring specialized service. Here is a task which has not been budgeted, projected, or provided for by existing mission agencies.

We welcome any other efforts or programs for meeting this need, and do not desire that this call for conference should halt any plans already inaugurated.

"When will the day come," exclaims a missionary writing of the Quichuas and Aymaras of Bolivia, "in which a great and powerful mission will begin its work of evangelizing these descendants of the lordly Incas, to bring them to Him, the King of Kings, Christ, their Savior?"(43)

The letter was signed by H. B. Dinwiddie of Philadelphia, B. F. Culp also of Philadelphia, Thomas Moffett of New York City, John Steele of Syracuse, Howard Kelly of Baltimore, Mr. and Mrs. J. Harvey Borton of New Jersey, Mrs. Walter Roe of Oklahoma, and L. L. Legters of Bishopville, South Carolina.

Dinwiddie sent copies to many denominational leaders as well as to Judge Scott and Luther Rees of the Central American Mission.

The conference went off splendidly. Some six denominations sent representatives; and, although the C.A.M. did not send Mr. Rees and Judge Scott, they sent Mr. Lange and Miss Gohrman as delegates, to show that they *were* concerned about the unreached ethnic groups of Latin America.

Dinwiddie, elated with the results, wrote Cam Townsend that "in every conclusion reached there was entire unanimity," and that "the Executive was one in desiring to carry out the vision born at Chichicastenango."(44)

A letter Dinwiddie wrote to Elvira Townsend, still under medical care at that time, gives further details about the Philadelphia conference:

> The same things were considered as at Chichicastenango with the same result . . . The conclusion reached was that it would be better to have the organization named a committee as that name "mission" has already been misunderstood as being a competitive agency to other mission work. Also the word "Latin" preceding America was very generally thought to have an element of offensiveness, as the Indians really have prior right in the territory in which they live. Consequently, the name that is to be suggested to the Guatemalan Field Council is that of the "Indian Mission Committee of America" which has met with unanimous approval here. The following members have been elected, and have signified their acceptance for what is called the Executive of the Committee. Dr. Thomas C. Moffett, Secretary of the Indian work of the Presbyterian Board of Home Missions, North. Mrs. Alfred R. Page, wife of Judge Page of the New York Supreme Court, member of the Dutch Reformed Church and very prominent and active in the Indian work of the Reformed Church of the United States; J. Harvey Borton, of the Society of Friends, Chairman of the Victorious Life Testimony, a rare man. Three or four other names have been proposed . . . (45)

A letter from Burgess to Robinson shows that the new Indian Mission Committee of America expected the L.A.I.M. officers elected at Chichicastenango to relinquish their status as the "L.A.I.M. General Council" and become instead merely one of several projected field committees:

I suppose you have had word from Bro. Dinwiddie in regard to the result of the Philadelphia Conference and the formation of the Indian Mission Committee of America. The suggestion has come that the Guatemala Field Council (now functioning as the General Council) of the Latin American Indian Mission should accept the new name and accept the status of Guatemala Field Committee of the Indian Mission Committee of America.(46)

In November 1921 a full report of the Philadelphia Conference was published.

After several paragraphs showing the extreme need in Latin America (for example, in Peru one section comprising fifteen thousand square miles was without a single missionary), the report made note of the following actions:

RESOLVED: That it is the sense of this meeting that the Indians of Central and South America and Mexico (in proportion to their total numbers) are the most neglected people in the world with respect to evangelical mission work, and that the present forces and methods employed are insufficient for their evangelization.

RESOLVED: That we express as the sense of this meeting that there is definite need of securing accurate information about the need of the Latin American Indian and for supplying that information to the Christian people of the United States . . .

After prayerful consideration of the great subject which has brought us into a united and blessed fellowship for the religious welfare of the Indians, humbly trusting that we have been led of God and are following His divine guidance, we do now organize the

"Indian Mission Committee of America"

with the purpose of evangelizing these long-neglected millions of the native race of Central and South America and Mexico.

The two-fold operation of the Committee shall be: First, as a Service Agency primarily to aid Mission Boards and Societies to meet this demand; Secondly, as a mission organization to reach these neglected people where these agencies are not undertaking or projecting this work.

The report went on to mention that the Executive had met September 28, with the following as officers:

Thomas Moffett—Chairman
H. B. Dinwiddie—General Secretary
L. L. Legters—Field Secretary
Mrs. Alfred Page—Recording Secretary
J. Harvey Borton—Treasurer

Additional members of the Executive were Mrs. J. Harvey Borton and Dr. Howard Kelly. Note was made of plans to make a survey trip through South America, and to absorb the members of the L.A.I.M.(47)

Thus we see that the L.A.I.M. was short-lived, for it merged with the Indian Mission Committee less than a year after being organized in Chichicastenango.

Nevertheless, the L.A.I.M. was extremely important, for it was in Chichicastenango that the vision was conceived. In the words of Dinwiddie, the officers of the Indian Mission Committee were united in desiring to carry out *the vision born at Chichicastenango*.

Several things about the Philadelphia Conference are worth noting:

1. Prayer played a strategic part.
2. Cooperation was stressed, and every effort was made to invite the leaders of denominational and independent agencies.
3. The Indian peoples were recognized as an unreached, neglected mission field.
4. There was a desire to reach South America as well as Central America and Mexico.
5. Evangelism and discipleship were emphasized. Bible translation, so strongly urged at Chichicastenango, was not mentioned, but note was made that the Indians should be evangelized in their own languages.
6. The Wycliffe Bible Translators' motto, "We pioneer," seems to be a direct echo of the thrust of the Philadelphia Conference.

Two questions arise as to the Committee formed in Philadelphia: 1. WHAT HAPPENED TO THE INDIAN MISSION COMMITTEE OF AMERICA? With that great, prayer-watered beginning, with that impressive list of executive board members, why does this organization not appear in the annals of mission history?

The Indian Mission Committee did continue to exist for at least twelve years. Its 1932 and 1933 letterhead shows that, even though Dinwiddie had died, the work was continuing. The word "Committee" had been dropped somewhere along the way, and THE INDIAN MISSION OF AMERICA had its headquarters at 80-82 Stafford Building, Philadelphia. Under FIELDS, the stationery reads: "The Neglected Native Indian Populations of the Americas and Mexico." Under OFFICERS are listed W. B. Coleman, Chairman; Thomas C. Moffett, D.D., Secretary; Rev. L. L. Legters, Field Representative; J. Harvey Borton, Treasurer; and Miss A. M. Vandiver, Recording Secretary. Thus it is evident that even after twelve years, the only members of the original Executive who were replaced were Rev. Dinwiddie and Mrs. Page.

During those twelve years, the Indian Mission Committee of America became primarily a fund-channeling agency. For example, monthly support for a Quiché evangelist named Marcelino Vásquez was sent regularly to Paul Burgess. Sometimes, when the Indian Mission Committee funds were low, the Pioneer Mission Agency transferred some of its undesignated gifts to the Indian Mission Committee so that this support could continue. After all, the agencies were geographically close (both in Philadelphia) and Mr. Borton, treasurer of the Indian Mission Committee, was also on the board of the Pioneer Mission Agency. Initially, both organizations had Leonard Legters as field secretary and Howard Dinwiddie as general secretary, or director. In recruiting candidates for the C.A.M. and other boards, these men sometimes used Indian Mission Committee stationery, but more often their letters appear on the stationery of the Pioneer Mission Agency.

Gradually, the Pioneer Mission Agency took over most of the functions of the Indian Mission Committee. And in time, new organizations sprang up to send out church planters and translators to "the neglected native Indian populations of the Americas and Mexico." The Indian Mission Committee of America ceased to exist.

The second question which may well be asked is: 2. IF THE INDIAN MISSION COMMITTEE OF AMERICA WAS SO SHORT-LIVED, WHY IS IT SIGNIFICANT? After all, many "fly-by-night" missions have been organized, have launched a work with great enthusiasm, and then have folded or have been absorbed by other agencies. Was not the Indian Mission Committee just one of these?

The significance of the Indian Mission Committee lies in the fact that it was an important link in a chain. The vision for a cooperative, large-scale effort to give minority ethnic groups God's Word in their own language was born in Chichicastenango. It became the Indian Mission Committee of America in Philadelphia. This organization in turn gave way to the Pioneer Mission Agency, which paved the way for the great work of the Summer Institute of Linguistics and the Wycliffe Bible Translators.

B. THE PIONEER MISSION AGENCY

Howard Dinwiddie had a remarkable gift for inspiring people and for organizing them into a team. In less than twelve months, he was involved in the founding of three organizations: The L.A.I.M., the Indian Mission Committee of America, and the Pioneer Mission Agency. A biographical sketch states:

> In 1921 Mr. Dinwiddie founded in Philadelphia the Pioneer Mission Agency, an organization which while not engaging directly in missionary work, cooperates with and assists other evangelical and missionary bodies, denominational and interdenominational, by investigating and suggesting new fields for missionary effort and as far as possible providing the missionaries and funds for undertaking it. (48)

The Pioneer Mission Agency was similar in many ways to its sister organization, the Indian Mission Committee. However, its base was somewhat broader, its geographical outreach went beyond the Americas, and its life was longer, for it still exists today, as a branch of Keswick.

An October 1921 letter from Dinwiddie to Luther Rees of the Central American Mission mentions the incorporation of both the Pioneer Mission Agency and the Indian Mission Committee of America, so it is probable that they were incorporated about the same time. Dinwiddie was the moving force behind both. So intense was he in his desire to raise up men and money for pioneer work that he wrote to Rees: "I have resigned from the directorate of all organizations not having to do with foreign missions."(49)

Shortly after the Pioneer Mission Agency was incorporated, an article in *The Sunday School Times* explained why such an organization was needed, and at the same time referred to its Student Volunteer roots:

> A score of years ago the cry was raised for the evangelization of the world in a single generation—in our generation. More than half of *that* generation has passed, counting a generation at thirty-three years. The world has by no means been evangelized, and in the little more than a decade of the generation that remains to be rounded out there is little likelihood, at the present rate of missionary progress, that the world will be fully evangelized in this remaining time. And the cry for the evangelization of the world in this generation seems no longer to be sounded out as it was some years ago, as when Arthur T. Pierson wrote "The Crisis of Missions" and John R. Mott, "The Evangelization of the World in this Generation."(50)

The article went on to say that because of the "untold multitudes of human souls for whom Christ died, but for whose immediate evangelization no provision has been made nor is even being contemplated by any of the existing missionary organizations," Dinwiddie and others had incorporated the Pioneer Mission Agency with the purpose "to learn and publish the need, and to forward workers and means, for pioneer mission work."

A list of the officers of the Pioneer Mission Agency reads

much like that of the Indian Mission Committee or the Victorious Life Testimony,

J. Harvey Borton, chairman, was president and general manager of the Haines, Jones and Cadbury Company, a corporation with factories and branches in several large cities. He was a godly man, active in the Society of Friends and the Victorious Life Testimony, and willing to use his economic resources and business acumen for the Lord.

His wife, *Alice Reed McClure Borton*, served on the boards of both the Pioneer Mission Agency and the Indian Mission Committee. Prior to her marriage to Mr. Borton, she had been a Presbyterian missionary in India, one of those who participated in the Punjab revival which gave birth to the New Wilmington Missionary Conference and to the Victorious Life Movement in the United States. She had also served as a traveling secretary of the Student Volunteer Movement.

B. F. Culp, treasurer of the Pioneer Mission Agency, was an elder in the Presbyterian Church and active in the Scripture Gift Mission as well as in the Victorious Life Testimony.

Howard Dinwiddie was elected general secretary and *L. L. Legters* was chosen as field secretary—positions identical to their roles in the L.A.I.M. and the Indian Mission Committee.

In addition, noted Bible teacher *Dr. W. H. Griffith-Thomas*, as well as *Rev. Charles G. Trumbull* and *Howard Banks*, both of *The Sunday School Times,* served on the board of the Pioneer Mission Agency.

The role of the Pioneer Mission Agency is better known than that of its sister organization, the Indian Mission Committee. Over the years, the leaders of the Pioneer Mission Agency sponsored survey trips into many remote parts of the world, recruited scores of men and women for pioneer mission work with other agencies, and channeled untold thousands of dollars into mission work. Many of these donations supported national evangelists who could witness and preach in their own non-European languages. Other gifts supported North American missionaries who engaged in pioneer work. During Wycliffe's early days, many of its members were supported through the Pioneer Mission Agency, until W.B.T. grew so large that it became logistically impossible for the Pioneer Mission Agency to continue this effort.

Another immense contribution of the Pioneer Mission Agency was the mighty army of prayer warriors raised up through the conference ministry of Dinwiddie and Legters.

One regiment of this army may be seen in the more than twenty individuals, recruited by Legters, who prayed regularly for Paul Burgess and the Quiché people. These persons not only prayed for the work, but they also sent monthly support for specific Quiché evangelists and influenced their churches and Sunday school classes in the U.S.A. to pray for the Indians. Just one example will show the tenor of many of the letters which Burgess received on a monthly basis from persons who had learned about his work through the conference ministry of Legters and Dinwiddie:

> As you know, the Indians, from Mexico to Cape Horn, are a heavy load on my heart, and I get impatient that so little is now done to meet their dire need.(51)

Dinwiddie and Legters recruited similar bands of praying men and women for the Townsends and the Cakchiquel evangelists and teachers, and for Herbert Toms and an Indian evangelist named Miguel Esteban who had an itinerant ministry in the province of Huehuetenango. When new pioneer missionaries, such as Dudley and Dorothy Peck, arrived on the field, the Pioneer Mission Agency recruited prayer partners for them also, and secured support for the Mam co-translators and evangelists in their area.

Only in God's records, perhaps, will be found the names of all the persons who were inspired by the lectures of Dinwiddie and Legters and who devoted themselves to prayer for the unevangelized Indian peoples. Many of them did not live to see the great surge of Bible translators penetrate these very tribes during the past few decades. Nor did they live to hear how large ethnic groups, which in the 1920s were without a single evangelical believer, have a high proportion of Christians in the 1990s! But surely the prayers and gifts of these named and unnamed individuals played a great part in reaching Latin America's minority groups.

Marguerite McQuilkin Cartee, in the biography of her father Robert C. McQuilkin, gives insight into the growth of a movement blessed by God:

> When one begins to investigate the converging influences in a given life or movement, one may follow a myriad of streams seeking to get back to the original source of blessing. But back and back one goes until one realizes that if human records were complete, every stream of blessing would be found to flow not only immediately, but historically as well, from the Fountain, the One who said, "If any man thirst let him come unto me and drink."(52)

She then traces one of the myriad streams of revival blessing. The All-Indian Prayer Circle in India gave birth to a Sialkot convention in that country. The Sialkot meetings resulted in the formation of the New Wilmington Missionary Conference. The New Wilmington Missionary Conference was the source of Trumbull's and McQuilkin's Victorious Life experience which in turn gave rise to the Victorious Life Testimony and America's Keswick.

To Mrs. Cartee's investigation of these "converging influences" we may add that the Victorious Life Testimony sent Dinwiddie to Guatemala. He, in turn, recruited his friend Legters for the Chichicastenango Conference where a new vision was born—the vision of a large-scale cooperative effort to reach minority language groups and to translate God's Word for them. The short-lived L.A.I.M., born at that conference, became the Indian Mission Committee of America and inspired the organization of the Pioneer Mission Agency. The Pioneer Mission Agency helped to found the original Camp Wycliffe at Sulphur Springs, Arkansas, in 1934. In fact, it was known as "The Pioneer Mission Agency's Training Camp" before it was called The Summer Institute of Linguistics.(53)

The Pioneer Mission Agency's Training Camp evolved into S.I.L. and the Wycliffe Bible Translators. And so the river of life flows on, and each year new peoples are able to read of God's offer of living water in words they can understand.

5

THE VISION SPREADS TO MEXICO

Howard Dinwiddie and Leonard Legters sailed to Guatemala in October 1921. They had every reason to feel enthusiastic. The Indian Mission Committee of America and the Pioneer Mission Agency were both functioning, support was being channeled to several national workers in Guatemala, and new recruits from North America were responding to the call for Indian work.

From aboard the *Saramacca*, a United Fruit Company steamship, Dinwiddie wrote to Luther Rees of the Central American Mission's Home Council:

> I am sorry that we did not meet. It seems to me that Satan is trying to create a lack of understanding between us. May God make us faithful one to another as members of the One Body of Christ. . . . Will you pray that God may make this trip into Honduras, Salvador and Guatemala, and Mexico, if God wills, a time of the same unbroken harmony, continued outpouring of the Spirit, that worked the last one; that native Christians may become soul winners, missionaries more clearly see their Lord, and Indians, tribe after tribe, may be located, hear the Gospel in their own language through messengers sent them, and the believers may be used to evangelize the rest of their tribe.(54)

Dinwiddie's enthusiasm, however, was dampened soon after he and Legters reached Guatemala. And in early December, at the annual C.A.M. conference in Guatemala City, he waged a personal battle against discouragement and depression. Both he and Legters were guests in the Bishop home, and

72

there they sensed a decided coolness toward their plans and dreams for Indian advance.

It seemed that the high hopes expressed in Chichicastenango eleven months earlier were about to be dashed to the ground. Cameron Townsend was in the United States looking after his sick wife, and some of his fellow C.A.M. missionaries were criticizing his policies in his absence.

Eleven months earlier Dinwiddie's heart had been knit to Townsend's in a remarkable way. Together they had scaled Volcano Agua and talked on the summit until the wee hours of the morning, sharing the great concern that consumed them both: the need of minority language groups to have God's Word in their own tongue.

But now Townsend was absent, and Dinwiddie missed his moral support and enthusiastic spirit. The older man expressed his feelings several months later in a poignant letter:

> Conditions were very confused politically and spiritually when I was in Guatemala, and no one seemed to share the desire expressed by you for the teaching among the Indians, or if they did, no one spoke of it. . . . As I wrote before, as you were away the bottom seemed to have dropped out of the Indian work.(55)

Due to a political uprising in Panajachel, Robinson was not able to attend the Guatemala City conference either. Burgess, too, was absent. And the Treichlers, enmeshed in a host of personal problems, appeared unresponsive and distant to Dinwiddie.

Furthermore, the majority of C.A.M. missionaries were concentrating on plans for the upcoming evangelistic campaign of Harry Strachan of Costa Rica and Juan Varetto of Argentina. No one seemed to have time to think about the needs of the republic's majority—the more than one million Indians who wouldn't even be able to understand the evangelistic sermons of the brilliant Argentine Baptist.

When would Dinwiddie be able to get the members of the L.A.I.M. together? And where would they meet? The Treich-

lers did not wish to host a second Indian conference in Chichicastenango. "There will not be beasts this time to send from
here for Mr. Dinwiddie and Mr. Legters, whereas they can get
to Quezaltenango without beasts," was the reason they gave.
(56)

Robinson wrote that he was eager "to arrange a conference of the Indian missionaries similar to that of last spring, together with a week or ten days of Bible studies for the Indian
workers," but he felt that he did not yet have enough space
available to host such a gathering.(57)

So it was decided that the Second Indian Conference
would be held in Quezaltenango, on February 5-12, 1922, with
Paul and Dora Burgess as hosts. Dinwiddie confirmed the dates
in a letter to Burgess, and then added:

> Perhaps it is not necessary to impress upon you our conviction
> of the very great importance of the part prayer plays in the prepara-
> tion for such a conference. As we clumsy foreigners are stripped by
> the process of interpretation of any but the more distinctively spiri-
> tual elements of our ministry, we are perhaps the more conscious of
> our need of prayer.(58)

While they were waiting for the Second Indian Conference, Dinwiddie and Legters held Victorious Life meetings in
eastern Guatemala and El Salvador and continued the survey of
tribes in that area which they had begun in the fall. They found
that there was not a single missionary for the Paya, Sumu, and
Sumbo tribes of Honduras, and neither was there any for the
45,000 Nahuat Indians of Sonsonate in El Salvador, whose language was related to Aztec.

From the Friends mission station at Chiquimula, Dinwiddie wrote to Burgess:

> We are gathering interesting information regarding the Spanish-
> speaking Indian of Southern Guatemala and El Salvador. Though
> Spanish is his common tongue he has been passed over in the evan-
> gelization of the missionaries almost as completely as the Indians
> that still speak their ancient tongues. . . . By the way, please invite
> Miss Smith [a Friends missionary] to send her Indian workers to the

Conference at Quezaltenango. Two of them are the first missionaries sent out from Guatemala in whose wake there have sprung up twenty congregations on the road to Tegucigalpa.(59)

After Legters and Dinwiddie returned from El Salvador and Chiquimula, the Second Annual Indian Conference convened in Quezaltengango. Although Burgess reported that "our conferences with Mr. Legters and the Indians were very worthwhile,"(60) neither the attendance nor the spirit of the gathering soared to the level reached at Chichicastenango the year before. Only some twelve Indians from Burgess' field and a scant three from Robinson's area attended the meetings.

Although Burgess had mailed invitations to every missionary who attended the Chichicastenango Conference, as well as to Dr. Thomas Moffett (chairman of the Indian Mission Committee of America) and to several others, only four field missionaries were present at the second conference: Paul and Dora Burgess, W. E. Robinson, and Albert Hines. The ranks were reduced to a fraction of the previous year's group.

Hines, a Pentecostal missionary from Totonicapán, accepted the invitation in the following way:

Replying to your general letter addressed to the members of the "Latin American Indian Mission" will say: Not being a member of the Mission nor knowing the nature of the proposed campaign we naturally have nothing to offer. . . . However, as to the spiritual welfare of the Indians . . . we are exceedingly interested. . . . We will be glad, therefore, to unite in prayer with you and them at the date and hour mentioned.(61)

Burgess had tried his best to rally the L.A.I.M. members to Quezaltenango, but the Townsends were in the U.S.A. and the Treichlers and Herbert and Mary Toms simply did not attend.

Nevertheless, the core of men and women who were truly committed to tribal work were determined that the vision born in Chichicastenango should not die. Although the flame was flickering, they would not let it go out. Not only must the Indians of Guatemala, El Salvador, and Honduras be reached; the tribes of Mexico must also be located and evangelized in their own tongues.

Townsend had spoken earlier of his longing to see Mexico's tribes reached. He had heard of 200,000 Mayas in British Honduras and Yucatán "where little if anything is known of the Gospel." He wasn't ready to leave the Cakchiquel field yet, but he felt restless, as though he knew that his whole life was not to be devoted merely to that one linguistic group. "My heart just burns to get the pioneering part of the work done in this section so as to be able to go to a more needy field," he wrote to Dinwiddie before he left San Antonio for his short furlough.(62)

Although Townsend was in the United States, Dinwiddie, Legters, and Burgess continued to ponder the need of locating and surveying the tribes of Mexico. Dinwiddie left Quezaltenango to attend to other engagements, but Legters stayed on after the Second Indian Conference, waiting for Burgess to recover from a high fever so that they could survey the Chiapas Indian situation together.

Hampered by not knowing Spanish or Quiché, Legters paced the floor, prayed, and amused the Burgess girls by producing rubber spiders or fake puddles of milk at the table.

Linn Sullenberger, who had taken over the Spanish work in Quezaltenango, conducted Legters up a steep mountain where they could visit the caves of witch doctors. As he saw them bending over the crude altars, burning *copal* incense and voicing centuries-old prayers to the spirits of the mountains, Legters felt his heart burn with a renewed desire to find recruits who could reach such people. This was his responsibility as field secretary for both the Pioneer Mission Agency and the Indian Mission Committee of America. But in order to raise up workers for the tribes, he needed *facts*.

As soon as Burgess recovered, he and Legters set off for Chiapas to survey its tribes and obtain those very facts.

"I'm Paul, we could call you Barnabas, and we're setting off on a missionary journey," suggested Burgess. "So let's call our mule John Mark."

The little mule was loaded with Bibles and tracts when the two men left on foot. During their six weeks on the road, they experienced imprisonment, stoning, and severe illness. At times they dared eat nothing except eggs boiled in their shells. Yet they found the information they were seeking.

Although eighty percent of the inhabitants of Chiapas were Indians, only thirty percent of these could speak Spanish. "These non-Spanish-speaking Indians have no less than sixty different languages and dialects of their own, all duly classified in the government census," Burgess reported in the widely read *Missionary Review of the World*.(63)

Burgess also reported a spiritual revival among the Spanish-speaking people of Chiapas. Congregations were springing up almost spontaneously, many of them without foreign missionary guidance. Mexican pastor José Coffin, a Presbyterian, had baptized 400 adults in one month.

But among the Indians the story was different. Although some Catholic priests, following the example of the early cleric Bartolomé de Las Casas, had learned the Indian languages, it was doubtful whether they had brought the true message of Christianity to the Indians. The long-haired, primitive Lacandón Indians, who still hunted with bows and arrows, were completely untouched by the gospel. But so were the thrifty, industrious highland tribes like the Tzeltals and the Tzotzils. Burgess and Legters concluded that if they were to be reached at all, they must be reached in their own language. Burgess continued in his article:

> The crying need of Chiapas is for missionaries to the Tzotzils and the Tzeltals. No Indian, so far as we could discover, has been won to the Gospel from either of these great tribes. The movement which has swept so many Ladinos to the Gospel has left these Indians untouched. Nor is it likely that an effort on the part of our Spanish-speaking brethren to evangelize them, would be very successful. The Ladinos have always been the exploiters of the Indians. . . . We were told semiofficially that the Government would welcome missionaries for the tribes. . . . May our Lord raise up an apostle to them as brave and loving and more enlightened than Las Casas.(64)

The 1922 trip through Chiapas was but the first of many such surveys made by Leonard Legters. A year later, he wrote in his cryptic style to Burgess:

> I have a lot of added information about the Indians added to what we got. The Zoque 90,000. 3500 of them speak Spanish. . . . Tzeltal about 30,000. A few speak Spanish. The Tzotzil: The census men told me they had enumerated only those in cities, pueblos and ranchos, that those in the mountains and out of sight were not counted, that there at least 125,000 to 200,000 of the tribe (Chamula) . . . That the least number of Lacandones is 36,000.(65)

From Oaxaca, he wrote: "Oaxaca is an *Indian* problem. Such as Guatemala cannot dream of."(66)

After he returned to Bishopville, South Carolina, he again wrote to Burgess, elaborating on his visit to Oaxaca and his contact with Presbyterian missionary L. P. Van Slyke, considered the apostle to the Zapotecs:

> Here are exact government figures on Presbyterian territory in Mexico. I do not agree on all of it [Legters felt that the government had underestimated the number of Indians] but it will give you something to pray for. Also Van Slyke. *He* is a dandy, is doing what you did, asking the board to release him for Indian work. I have offered to pay his expenses if he will visit your work and Townsend. He feels the need of seeing *how* you all do the work. You will love him . . . *Eats* up languages. . . .

The number who *do no*t speak Spanish:

Yucatán	1 tribe	200,073
Veracruz	10 tribes	198,098
Tabasco	1 tribe	11,956
Oaxaca	14 tribes	507,283
Chiapas	8 tribes	120,163
Campeche	1 tribe	28,280(67)

The many surveys which Legters carried out both in Mexico and in South America had a profound effect upon the linguistic work and evangelism which is being done in Latin America today.

It was Legters who later challenged Cameron Townsend

to begin his Summer Institute of Linguistics in Mexico rather than in South America, reminding him that the tribes of Mesoamerica were far larger than those along the Amazon.

It was Legters who influenced his own son Brainerd to devote his life to the large Maya tribe of Yucatán, to translate the New Testament into their language, and to develop churches, camps, and Christian leaders among the Mayas.

It was Legters who persuaded a college student named Ed Sywulka to go to Guatemala rather than South America if he wanted to find large groups of Indians. It was Legters who challenged young Ken Pike, rejected by the China Inland Mission, with the opportunity to prepare himself to become a translator for Mexico's tribes. It was Legters who helped to channel young Bill Hays and his bride into Quiché work under the Primitive Methodist Board.

Who knows exactly how many other young people were led into Bible translation because of the influence of Legters and his surveys? The list could go on and on! Some of his recruits are still actively engaged in Indian work today; a number of them have translated the New Testament into more than one language.

And the very tribes for which Legters and Burgess felt such a great burden in 1922—the Tzotzils and the Tzeltals—began to be reached for Christ some twenty years later. By the time the Tzeltal New Testament was completed by Wycliffe translator Marianna Slocum and her co-workers in 1956, there were more than a thousand Tzeltal evangelicals, and today there is a very strong church in the region. This church is a tribute to the faithful, persevering work of Slocum and her companions. At the same time, however, it is a tribute to the prayers of a host of men and women, known only to God, who began to pray for the tribes of Chiapas in 1922, after hearing or reading the reports of Burgess and Legters.

6

THE ROBINSON BIBLE INSTITUTE

Cameron Townsend was eager to see the Indian work progress in all areas: health ministries and education as well as translation. He established the Louise Heim Clinic in San Antonio Aguas Calientes in 1921, and soon after he obtained the help of Dr. and Mrs. H. A. Becker, experienced medical missionaries who devoted themselves to ministering to the sick as well as to evangelizing the Cakchiquel Indians.

The educational need of the Indians was another concern which Townsend shared with Dinwiddie and the rest of the "Chichicastenango Twelve." The Townsends had already begun an elementary school for Cakchiquel Indian children. But there was still the need of an institute to train pastors and church leaders.

The first step was to launch some short-term training efforts. The Dinwiddie-Legters conferences held in San Antonio, Chichicastenango, and Quezaltenango in 1921 included sessions for national workers as well as for English-speaking missionaries. Then Townsend sent five laymen from his field to a Workers' Institute in Huehuetenango. This was a short-term Bible school, directed by Frank Toms and his son Herbert, which met for two or three months each summer. Classes were taught in Spanish, but Indian students were welcomed.

When the Cakchiquel men returned from Huehuetenango, Townsend realized that they would have learned far more if the classes had been taught in their own language. So he began his own short-term Institute for Cakchiquel Indians. The first sessions, taught by Townsend and Robinson, were held just before Townsend left for the United States in the fall of 1921. Over fifteen young men signed up to spend nine days a month in concentrated Bible study at Panajachel.

During Townsend's absense, Robinson continued to teach these sessions and expanded them into a very successful four-week course.

The other members of the "Chichicastenango Twelve" were also backing the idea of an Indian Bible School at Panajachel. Burgess promised to send students and to help out with the teaching. And Dinwiddie, who lived "by faith" on a very frugal budget, sacrifically donated $300 to Robinson for the purchase of a property and the construction of buildings.

Robinson wrote elatedly:

> With the construction of the home, the school and the chapel, all of which have been started, we believe that the Lord will have given us a splendid center for His service. (68)

In addition to supervising the construction and teaching the Bible classes, Robinson continued to engage in evangelism. At times he visited two or three villages in one day, with two Cakchiquel preachers interpreting his messages.

In February 1922 Townsend returned to Guatemala, barely missing the Second Indian Conference at Quezaltenango. At this time he was eager not only to make progress on the translation, but also to set up a permanent Bible school. He felt strongly that Dinwiddie, with his gift for Bible teaching, would be just the man for such a school. The following letter is just one among many in which Townsend tried to persuade Dinwiddie to cut loose from his homeland duties and give full time to training Indians:

> You don't know how a man of your gifts is needed right here on the field. I believe that if we could train systematically by conferences and Bible classes even only the Indian believers of this and Burgess' district, that God would raise up from their midst sufficient workers to evangelize all the Indians of Central America. Funds are

81

not our great need. We need men filled with the Spirit to preach the
Gospel and to teach the converts. Of course God can use you to interest others but it seems to me that the marked degree in which He
used you when you were here among our Indians the other time
would show a strong possibility that He has called you to minister
directly to their needs. (69)

Dinwiddie, however, felt just as strongly that he was needed in the *homeland* to raise recruits and support for Indian
work. Furthermore, after his experience with controversy within both the Africa Inland Mission and the Central American
Mission home councils, he did not wish to join the C.A.M. as a
missionary.

Townsend realized, therefore, that he would not be able to
count on Dinwiddie as a teacher at the Bible School which he
and Robinson envisioned. But he knew that he *could* count on
Dinwiddie's prayers and moral support as he went ahead with
plans for the Institute.

In June 1922 Townsend responded to Robinson's invitation to spend a few days with him in his new lakeside home,
called "Beulah." Robinson's wife was away for a few days visiting a plantation, and the two men planned to spend a week or
ten days in concentrated language study. They also intended to
devote themselves to prayer and to planning how they would
open the Bible School they had envisioned for Panajachel.

But the week of prayer, study and planning never material-
ized. While the two buddies were swimming on their first day
together at the lake, Townsend saw Robinson reach upward,
shake his head, and then go under. By the time he reached his
friend, Townsend had seen him slip down for the third time.
After a difficult struggle, Robinson's body was finally brought
to the shore. Artificial respiration proved futile, for he had suffered a cerebral hemorrhage.

Although grief-stricken himself, Townsend opened his
Spanish Bible to John 11 and began to read Christ's words of
hope to the astonished onlookers who had gathered at the
scene. Then he sent telegrams to break the news to Robinson's
co-workers and loved ones.

The Treichlers received their telegram in Chichicastenango that evening. They dropped everything they were doing, traveled all night, and reached Panajachel by morning, ready to help Townsend with the funeral arrangements and to comfort Mrs. Robinson as soon as she would arrive.

Genevieve Robinson's telegram took longer to reach her. A brief glance was enough to tell her that she was no longer a young bride, but rather a widow. To reach Panajachel in time for her husband's funeral, she spent eighteen hours riding a mule to the far shore of the lake that had claimed his life. Her host at the plantation escorted her all the way. Arriving at the port of Atitlán just before dark, she found that Louise Treichler had been waiting there for her since early that morning, ready to accompany her the rest of the way to Panajachel in a boat which had been sent for that purpose.

The funeral was held early the following day. Panajachel's mayor declared a day of mourning. Public school was suspended, and the school building was used for the service. The town orator, although not a Protestant, stated, "Panajachel has lost its greatest citizen. He had great plans for this entire district. The work must not stop; surely someone will come to continue it."

Trinidad Bac, a Cakchiquel pastor, preached the funeral sermon. "Robinson's coming marked a new day for the Indians," he said. "He gave us the Good News and helped to turn us from superstition to the true God. You say our friend Robinson is dead. That's not true! He is alive in heaven with God right now!"

Burgess, although unable to attend the funeral, felt Robinson's loss keenly. Very few missionaries had devoted themselves to the Indians, and now there was one fewer! He wrote to his mother: "This has left Mr. Townsend and us to carry on the Indian work about alone." (70)

In spite of his demanding schedule, Burgess gave a week that November to help Townsend with the translation of the Cakchiquel New Testament. Ben Treichler, too, was willing to help out temporarily. He wrote:

Mr. Townsend and I expect to share the responsibility of the work
Brother Robinson has worked into such good shape until someone
comes to take its direction off our hands. (71)

Dinwiddie also responded with sorrow to the news of Robinson's death. Yet even though there was such a desperate need for someone to take over the Bible School work which Robinson had begun, Dinwiddie was still sure that he was not the man to do it. He was called to recruit other laborers, and he knew that God would raise up the right person for the school.

One of the first men God provided was Archer Anderson, a Presbyterian and a graduate of the Philadelphia School of the Bible, who came to Guatemala under the Central American Mission and was assigned to work with the Townsends.

Anderson had read an article in which Townsend pleaded for help in establishing a Bible School for the Indians. "What has been done about that?" he asked after he arrived in Guatemala.

"We've been praying about it," answered Townsend. "I guess God has sent you!"

Townsend then took Anderson to Panajachel, and in March 1923, on the front porch of the lake-front home which Robinson had so recently built, the two men made bold plans to fulfill the unfinished dream and to establish a formal Bible training school for the tribes of Guatemala. They would call it *EL INSTITUTO BIBLICO ROBINSON* in honor of the man who had first envisioned it.

The two missionaries immediately began renovating the building which Robinson had purchased for the school with Dinwiddie's gift. Six weeks later, classes opened officially with some fifteen students.

Elvira Townsend taught music, Cameron Townsend led the chapel services and some of the classes, and Archer Anderson taught other classes, with Cameron interpreting for him. Before long, Anderson was conversing in both Spanish and Cakchiquel, and Townsend told him, "Andy, you'll be taking over all the classes by July. And by August, you'll be teaching in Cakchiquel!"

From the beginning, the Robinson Bible Institute was designed to serve not just the Cakchiquel field, but other tribes as well. Its doors were open to Indians of any Protestant denomination. Churches from the Presbyterian, Primitive Methodist, and Nazarene fields, as well as the churches of the Central American Mission, sent young people to study in its halls. By 1953, the school had functioned for thirty years, 300 students had been enrolled, ninety-nine had been graduated, and sixty-seven were serving as pastors and church lay leaders. Seven Guatemalan tribes and one from Mexico were represented in the student body. (72)

The Robinson Bible Institute began as a cooperative work. Even though most of the missionaries and nationals on the faculty were associated with the Central American Mission, members of other agencies were also invited as teachers. Paul Burgess came regularly for short periods to teach doctrine or church history while his wife Dora taught music. Edward Haymaker of the Presbyterian Mission was also invited to teach.

In 1953, the Institute celebrated its thirtieth anniversary with a week of special meetings. Twelve hundred Indians gathered to hear Cameron Townsend bring the graduation message in the Cakchiquel language. Then a half-mile long parade of believers marched four abreast through the town, singing as they went, until they reached the cemetery and held a memorial service at the grave of W. E. Robinson.

Even at that time, mission leaders were considering moving the school to a larger city. In time, the Robinson Bible Institute was moved to Chimaltenango, a provincial capital about an hour's drive from Guatemala City. Later, its name was changed to the Guatemala Bible Institute. Some Indians who still remembered Robinson were opposed to the name change. They remembered Townsend's buddy as a pioneer colporteur who walked the trails, his pack of Scriptures on his back, evangelizing the people whom he met along the paths. "That is the example we want our young men to follow," said the older Indians. "Don't take the name Robinson away from the school."

But the Institute's name was changed, and so was its purpose. In the 1990s, it serves to train Spanish-speaking young men and women, rather than Indians. Other separate Bible schools have been established for the Indians in their own tongues, so that a central school for all the tribes is no longer needed. Nevertheless, the impact of the Robinson Bible Institute—a school which grew out of the vision of the "Chichicastenango Twelve"—can still be felt throughout Guatemala as its graduates, and the church leaders whom they have trained, continue to spread the Good News and make disciples.

7

THE PRESBYTERIANS CATCH THE VISION FOR INDIAN WORK

Roughly speaking, the decade of 1922-1932 was marked by a tremendous surge of interest in Indian work on the part of mission boards which were already working in Guatemala or which were just entering the country. Prior to this time, the prevailing attitude of field missionaries, mission agencies (including the Presbyterian Board of Foreign Missions), and national church leaders was, "Don't use the tribal languages. Let the Indians learn Spanish and become a part of our Spanish churches."

Mexico's Dr. Gonzalo Báez Camargo, that erudite Christian man of letters, expressed the sentiments of many church leaders in a paper called *The Evangelization of the Indian Races*, which he presented at an Evangelical Congress in Havana in 1929:

> It is estimated that there are over eighty great linguistic trunks in all Latin America, each trunk being subdivided into a multitude of smaller branches or dialects. Antonio Peñafiel has counted fifty-five languages in Mexico alone. Most of these languages and dialects are in a primitive state....
>
> In respect to our work, it may be that some people will be inclined to evangelize in the native tongue. This would mean having to create, in the first place, a grammar for each language and dialect, since most of them have none; and secondly, ... having to reduce the language to writing in Latin characters. Then it would be necessary to translate the Scriptures into each language, and to give

each language its own special literature. This would cause the Indians to cling more than ever to their own dialects as their only means of expression, and would delay their incorporation into the national life. Apart from the immensity of such a labor, this would mean regression rather than progress....

The solution which we propose may be summarized as follows:

1) Our mission stations should make a vigorous effort to establish the national language among the Indians.

2) Every effort to produce a special literature in the native languages should be abandoned.

3) While the Indians are learning the national language... the preaching of the Gospel in their own tongue should be exclusively oral in form.

4) We do recommmend that Christian workers learn the native dialects sufficiently to use them as a means of contact and of psychological penetration. The study of language sheds much light upon each people's idiosyncrasies.

5) We should not wait until the missionaries learn the native language before beginning the work. This may be done through interpreters.

6) As the Indians make progress in learning the national language, the use of the native tongues for evangelization should be diminished.

7) We should give special attention to teaching the national language to the children. (73)

Professor Báez Camargo's views were shared by many other Christian leaders. This attitude, however, gradually gave place to a positive recognition of the importance of reaching the Indians in their own tongues. The field missionaries were the first to see how vital was this ministry. Then the boards began to catch the vision for tribal work and Bible translation.

Thus far *Trailblazers for Translators* has sought to explore the significance of the 1921 Chichicastenango conference, to shed some light upon the lives of the twelve persons who convened at that time, and to show how various organizations developed out of that gathering.

The remaining chapters are devoted to tracing the story of

how the mission boards which were working in Guatemala caught the vision which was "born in Chichicastenango." We will go back to the time when that mission agency entered Guatemala. We will explore briefly the board's initial policy toward Indian work, its change of policy, and its continued efforts in Indian evangelism and translation. Chapter Seven deals with the Presbyterians.

A. Initial Work.

The first Protestant mission agency to enter Guatemala was the Board of Foreign Missions of the Presbyterian Church in the U.S.A. In 1882, at the request of Guatemalan President Justo Rufino Barrios, they sent the Rev. John Hill to Guatemala City. Five years later, Hill was succeeded by Edward Haymaker, whose pioneer work in evangelism, literature and church planting laid the foundation for the phenomenal growth of Protestantism in that country which has continued up to the present time. Paul Burgess said of Haymaker:

> All the missions and missionaries held him in high esteem and the national brethren loved him as a father. He, more than any other, can be considered the Apostle of the Gospel in Guatemala. (74)

From the start, Haymaker was a staunch advocate for Indian evangelism and the use of Indian languages by missionaries; and he spoke out boldly against those who promoted Indian subservience and the perpetuation of the inhumane conditions in which they lived.

In 1919 Haymaker wrote and published a tract entitled "The Indians of Guatemala." In a flare of optimism he implied that the evangelization of the Mayan peoples would impact not only the future of the church of Guatemale, but also the spread of the Gospel throughout the entire world. His words proved to be prophetic, for it was among Indians of Mayan stock that the great modern Bible translation movement began.

In Haymaker's early ministry, he made a brief attempt to learn Quiché and translate some Scriptures. Although he was unable to continue this effort, he strongly influenced Walker

McBath, who also attempted to reach Guatemala's Indians for Christ.

Walker Eugene McBath arrived in Guatemala in 1903 under the Presbyterian Board. With Haymaker as his mentor, McBath organized Quezaltenango's large Bethel Church and purchased its present building site.

In 1906 McBath married Anne Alloway of the Central American Mission. Together, they dreamed of establishing a Bible and agricultural school for the Indians. Yet at that time, as we have noted, the Presbyterian Board insisted that the Indians become integrated into the Spanish culture. The McBaths saw this as a hopeless policy, resigned from the mission, and in 1913 moved to the Quiché village of Almolonga near Quezaltenango to begin work as independent missionaries

Here Walker and Anne taught Bible classes and vegetable gardening to the Indians. They were so successful in this endeavor that today Almolonga probably exports more vegetables to Guatemala City than any other community.

Unfortunately, the McBaths were forced to leave the country due to inadequate financial support. It remained for Paul and Dora Burgess to become the first Presbyterian missionaries in Guatemala to be assigned specifically to Indian work.

B. Quiché Work.

Although the Presbyterian board was at first hesitant to release Paul Burgess from his Spanish and German church duties, he was given the green light for Indian work less than a year after the historic 1921 Chichicastenango Conference. From then on, Presbyterian leaders in the New York headquarters were unabashedly enthusiastic about Indian outreach. Board Secretary Stanley White wrote in a general letter in 1923:

> The Guatemala Mission will be, I am sure, interested in certain things that have been happening lately relative to Indian work. There are a number of organizations that seem at the present time, to be particularly interested, not only the Committee of which Mr.

Dinwiddie is a member, but the Board of the Missionary Alliance [today known as the Christian and Missionary Alliance] and last week I had visits from several individuals who were eager to study and work among the Indians.... It is indicative it seems to me, of the fact that people are beginning to wake up to the spiritual needs of these various Indian tribes. (75)

Although Paul and Dora Burgess had begun to translate hymns and Scriptures into Quiché before being assigned to Indian work, they devoted themselves even more earnestly to translation after Mr. and Mrs. Linn Sullenberger returned to Quezaltenango to relieve them of the Spanish work. Paul Burgess' 1923 diary shows that he devoted many days to translating John's Gospel, in consultation with Quiché co-translators and with Amos Bradley of the Primitive Methodist Mission. During that year, the consultation was carried out in Totonicapán, at Bradley's home.

In 1924, Paul, who had never enjoyed robust health, became so ill that his doctors sent him to a sanatorium in Colorado. While he was gone, his wife Dora took up the translation, and literally fell in love with the Quiché language. By the time Paul returned to Guatemala with improved health, he knew that the translation was Dora's "baby," and he left her in charge of it, serving only as her consultant. From then on, the translation work was done in the Burgess home rather than the Bradley home.

The Quiché Gospel of John was printed on Burgess' second-hand pedal press in 1924. The salaries of the co-translators were paid by Mr. R. H. Young of Bradenton, Florida, a donor raised up by L. L. Legters; and the publishing costs were met by the American Bible Society. The demand for this Gospel was so great that within a year a second edition had to be printed.

The Quiché edition of Acts was published in 1926, and Matthew's Gospel followed shortly; both were printed on Burgess' press.

Dora Burgess translated from the original Greek, seeking

to express its sense in the purest, most classical Quiché possible. She used borrowed Spanish expressions only when absolutely necessary. Several Quiché men served as language consultants; foremost among these was Patricio Xec, who also helped Dora translate the ancient Quiché *Popol Vuj* into Spanish.

Because Dora was such a perfectionist, and because of sick leaves, family emergencies, and other missionary duties, as well as delays caused by World War II, it was 1946 before the complete Quiché New Testament came off the presses of the American Bible Society in New York, and 1947 before copies were shipped to Guatemala.

In 1941, the Burgesses established the Quiché Bible Institute to train young Quiché men and women for Christian service. Although the board at first approved the school only as an "experiment" without financial backing, they later not only sponsored the Institute financially, but also sent additional missionaries as teachers. Stanley Wick and his first wife Betty arrived in Guatemala in 1947, were assigned to the Quiché Bible Institute, and rapidly mastered the Indian language. In time, Wick became the outstanding director of this school. Another Presbyterian missionary who learned Quiché was Gail Maynard (later Gail Wick); her translations of didactic materials and Old Testament portions into Quiché have been greatly valued.

A revision of Dora Burgess' New Testament, produced by Wycliffe translator David Henne, was published in 1973. Updated translations of the New Testament for other Quiché dialects are being developed by Wycliffe personnel.

Before her death in 1962, Dora Burgess translated Genesis and Exodus into Quiché. Stan Wick and his co-workers continued translating the Pentateuch.

Stan Wick, who retired from Guatemala in 1979, and his second wife Gail maintained a continued interest in the translation work. Meanwhile, Patricio Xec kept on translating the Old Testament.

In Dr. and Mrs. James Cockings, Plymouth Brethren medical missionaries, Xec found kindred spirits who could help him continue this endeavor. Dr. Cocking, his wife, and Xec finished translating the Quiché Old Testament when Xec was past eighty years of age.

The lengthy process of checking the translation then began. This was carried out by the consultants of the United Bible Societies and members of the Wycliffe Bible Translators. By 1995, the entire Quiché Bible was being printed on a South Korean press, and the believers were looking forward to receiving the Bible shipment.

Paul Burgess dreamed for many years of organizing the Quiché Indian churches into an autonomous presbytery of their own. Nevertheless, the Maya-Quiché Presbytery was not organized until 1959, a year after Burgess' death. In 1982, 100 years after the first Presbyterian missionary set foot in Guatemala, this presbytery had grown to include sixteen fully organized churches and twenty congregations, with a grand total of 5,361 Quiché-speaking members.

C. Mam Work.

The Mams, along with the Quiché and Cakchiquel peoples, are ranked among Guatemala's three largest tribes.

Presbyterian work among the Mams began in San Juan Ostuncalco, a small town near Quezaltenango. Prior to 1911, a few influential Spanish-speaking residents of San Juan were converted. Walker McBath may have visited them and held services there.

In 1911 Presbyterian missionary Linn Sullenberger held services in San Juan, but it was not until February 17, 1914, that Paul Burgess organized the believers into an official congregation with eight charter members. Between 1914 and 1916, a handful of Mam Indians were converted and began attending the Spanish-speaking congregation which Burgess had organized.

And so, from the start of his missionary career, Burgess

was concerned for the Mams. In January of 1916 he wrote the American Bible Society urging them to sponsor a translation of the New Testament into Mam. He felt that he knew just the man to do the translating: Juan de Dios Castillo, a brilliant lawyer, one of the charter members of Quezaltenango's Bethel Church, and a man who had grown up among the Mam Indians and mastered their tongue since childhood.

Over a year went by before Burgess received an answer. The Bible Society wanted more information. How many readers were there in the Mam tribe? Was Mam closely enough related to Quiché or to Cakchiquel so that the 1902 editions of Scripture portions in those languages would suffice? John Fox of the American Bible Society closed his inquiry by saying:

> Please do not suppose that we are not sympathetic to your wishes. We would like to put the Bible or the New Testament, or a Gospel into every language that by any possibility could be used by even a small number of people, but we have so many demands for languages of great importance where there is a good prospect of it being used and our funds just now are so drawn on, that we are obliged to ask these questions. (76)

Burgess responded immediately with an impassioned plea for a Mam translation. He explained that the 1902 editions of Quiché and Cakchiquel Scriptures were not understood in his area, due "to the translation being made very carelessly and also to the great diversity of dialects in these languages." Nevertheless, he explained, even if the Quiché portions could be understood by the Quiché people, it would not help the Mams out:

> There is a very great difference between the Quiché and Cakchiquel languages and the Mam.... Even the common household words are entirely different. The difference between the two languages is greater than that between English and German or English and Spanish. If you care to look up the matter in more detail you will find some illuminating facts in some of the bulletins of the Bureau of American Ethnology in Washington. (77)

Burgess then went on to say that Mam was spoken "with

very few variations by about 200,000" people, and that about 15,000 of these could read Spanish phonetically and would therefore be able to read privately and publicly a Mam translation "which they would understand much better than Spanish." He continued:

> At present the work of evangelization has done little to reach this particular tribe... A version of the Word of God in their own tongue would undoubtedly stimulate the work among them wonderfully and lead to the gathering of many more souls into the Kingdom. (78)

It was late 1917 before Burgess received an answer:

> .... Am sorry it has been so long between letters, but it has been impossible to do differently. The matter of the Mam translation was taken up and carefully considered by our Versions Committee at a recent meeting and they came to the conclusion that a translation properly made in this language, of a single Gospel, experimentally, possibly a Diglot (Spanish and Mam) would be desirable, but in the present state of our funds it was scarcely prudent for us now to begin such a thing. (79)

John Fox also wanted to know whether the Mams were likely to take up Spanish in the near future, and whether Juan de Dios Castillo would be able to make his translation from the original Greek.

Burgess replied that there was no immediate prospect of the Mams giving up their native tongue, and that Castillo and his helpers would have to make the translation from the Spanish Bible rather than from the Greek. He added:

> I would be very glad, however, to cooperate with them explaining the significance of the Greek to them in Spanish and though my knowledge of Mam would not warrant my making or even supervising the translation, I understand enough to be sure whether the sense of the original is expressed or not. (80)

The United States, however, was at war, and the Bible Society was still short of funds. So the matter of the Mam Scriptures was dropped.

Interest in the Mams, however, was reawakened at the

1921 Chichicastenango Indian Conference. Part of the Mam territory lay in the province of Huehuetenango, where the Toms family was serving. Herbert Toms shared with Dinwiddie and Legters the great need of the Mams in his field, while Burgess spoke of the Mams residing in the territory assigned to the Presbyterian Mission.

When Dinwiddie returned to the United States, he had the Mam tribe on his heart, and he did two things for them. First, he began channeling support from donors in the United States to Herbert Toms for the purpose of supporting two Mam evangelists in Huehuetenango. Secondly, he actively sought to recruit missionary candidates for this language group.

Shortly after establishing the Indian Mission Committee of America and the Pioneer Mission Agency, Dinwiddie was invited to speak at Princeton Seminary. There he met young Horace Dudley Peck, a man who had been strongly influenced by the Student Volunteer Movement and who had hoped to work among the Indians of the United States. However, the Presbyterian Board of Home Missions had no opening for him in that field, and so its leaders were trying to steer him into applying for Spanish work in South America. But when he heard Dinwiddie tell of the great need of Guatemala's Mam Indians, Peck knew just what he must do: apply to the Board of Foreign Missions for that work.

Dudley Peck and his wife Dorothy arrived on the field in the fall of 1922. Paul Burgess wrote:

> We are so happy to have Mr. and Mrs. Peck sent to ... undertake work among the Mam Indians. At last it would seem that some provision is being made to give these poor Indians the Gospel.(81)

Dudley Peck proved to be exactly the kind of missionary Dinwiddie dreamed of sending out. He was determined to identify himself with the Indians in every possible way. His wife, a graduate of an exclusive women's college, was also willing to exchange her refined way of life for the simple patterns of the Mams. They rented a humble home for twenty-five cents a month, and they adopted Indian dress. They continued to rent native houses for eighteen years, until some enemy witch doctors burned their dwelling. After that, the Pecks built a mission center in San Juan Ostuncalco which included a home, a clinic and a Mam Bible Institute. Here they lived for most of the remainder of their nearly fifty years on the field. They retired from Guatemala in December 1969.

The Pecks began using the Mam language immediately, and soon they were translating the New Testament. Dorothy Peck proved to be the more gifted linguist in the family, and she worked steadily at her task. On their first furlough, the Pecks studied linguistics at Harvard, and Dorothy wrote:

> While nobody here knows any Mam, Dr. Tozzer, the head of the Anthropology Department, has written a Mayan grammar and Dr. Dixon, with whom we are working in this course, knows twenty languages, and gives us notable suggestions for scientific work. After we dig out the Mam grammar, we are to compare it with the other twenty-one languages of the Mayan stock. (82)

Thus, Dorothy Peck was possibly better trained in linguistics at that time than either Cameron Townsend or Dora Burgess, the other two missionaries who were devoting themselves to Bible translation in Guatemala in the 1920s.

By 1937, the Presbyterian Board definitely felt "proud and grateful" to have two couples—the Burgesses and the Pecks—engaged in pioneer Bible translation for the Indians of Latin America. In interdenominational gatherings, Presbyterian leaders could say, "Look what our missionaries are doing!" These leaders expressed their appreciation to the Guatemala-based missionaries:

> It is a matter for great rejoicing to know that ... the New Testament in the Mam tongue has been put on the press. The first draft of the Quiché New Testament has also been practically finished.... In any conference as to work being done by evangelical missionaries among the native peoples of Latin America, which is admittedly of almost a negligible quantity, as compared with other work, we are always glad to point with pride to that which is being done by our

97

Guatemala Mission. Other boards and groups are cognizant of what you are doing and appreciate very much the lead that you are thus taking in a very important work. (83)

The Mam New Testament was dedicated in 1940—the second New Testament to be published in a Guatemalan Indian language. (Actually, the Pecks finished their translation before Cameron Townsend completed his Cakchiquel New Testament. But because they later decided to revise it so as to make it more intelligible to all the Mam dialects, its publication was delayed until after that of the Cakchiquel translation.) Edward Haymaker commented about the Pecks' achievement:

They have done a good job. They are getting the Bible to them in a form that can be read in all twenty-one dialects of the Mams. This translation in addition to its main spiritual job will doubtless have the same effect on the Mam language as did the King James, Lutheran and Cherokee translations on their respective tongues—it must unify and stabilize them. (84)

The Pecks gave to the Mam churches not only the New Testament, but also a Bible Institute, Sunday school lessons, literacy materials, and a hymnbook with over 200 hymns.

Later, the Presbyterian Board assigned additional missionaries to the Mam Indians. Among these were Ruth Wardell, a tireless nurse and teacher who worked among the Mams for thirty years. Ralph and Roberta Winter, assigned to the Mam Center from 1957 to 1966, established the "Abraham Lincoln" school in their area and pioneered in the field of theological education by extension, before returning to the United States to found the U.S. Center for World Mission dedicated to the reaching of the world's hidden peoples.

David and Sara Scotchmer were recruited by Ralph and Roberta Winter at Fuller Theological Seminary. After ten weeks at the Summer Institute of Linguistics in Norman, Oklahoma, the Scotchmers arrived among the Mams in 1969. An extensive three-weeks language orientation, provided by Ed Sywulka, was followed by a year's residence in the Mam-speaking village of Varsovia at the urging of Ralph Winter.

Weekly visits with the Pecks gave the Scotchmers further cultural orientation.

The Scotchmers' work included the organization of three new Mam churches, training thirty Mam seminary graduates through an extension program and the founding of the Mam Presbytery in 1980. A literacy program, a health program for women, and a potable water project were also fruits of their thirteen years of missionary service.

Church growth among Presbyterian Mams has been steady and significant. By 1982, when Guatemala celebrated its centennial of Protestant mission work, the recently organized Mam Presbytery counted 3,068 persons as members of its churches. By 1994 the Mam Presbytery had grown to include eleven churches, ten pastors, and 5,000 members. The Presbyterian Mams run their own clinic, social service work, seminary program, and evangelistic outreach.

CAM's Ed Sywulka had such a good reputation as a careful translator that in 1970 the Presbyterians asked him to revise the Pecks' Mam New Testament. This edition, for many reasons, turned out to be a fresh translation rather than a simple revision.

Sywulka's partner in this effort was Rubén Díaz, a gifted Mam Indian trained by the Winters. The New Testament in the Ostuncalco dialect of Mam, translated jointly by Ed Sywulka and Rubén Díaz in just twenty-one months, has gone through two printings.

In 1980 David Scotchmer and Rubén Díaz began a translation of the Old Testament into Ostuncalco Mam, completing a rough draft of Genesis and Exodus. The translation was interrupted when the Scotchmers left Guatemala in 1982 for doctoral studies in Albany, New York, but was continued when David came in contact with a Mam family living in exile in Vermont. For three years, David worked weekly with them on Old Testament translation. This effort was supported jointly by the Presbyterian Church and the United Bible Societies.

By 1994, the entire Old Testament in Ostuncalco Mam

was being checked and revised. Genesis and Exodus were scheduled for publication in late 1994 and Psalms and Proverbs for early 1995. Pedro Daniel Cabrera, a gifted Mam pastor, directed the work and Ed Sywulka assisted with checking and revision.

Today's continued growth in Presbyterian churches among the once-hidden Quiché and Mam peoples can be traced directly to the vision of the "Chichicastenango Twelve." Going even further back, this church growth can be traced to the early vision of Haymaker and McBath who saw the need for distinctively Indian work, and who were bold enough to stand against the prevailing mission policies.

The dreams of Haymaker and McBath came to fuition in the ministry of "Chichicastenango Twelve" members Paul and Dora Burgess. It was this dedicated couple who gave the Scriptures to the Quiché tribe and then passed the torch of Quiché Bible translation on to people like the Wicks and Patricio Xec.

Howard Dinwiddie, another key figure among the "Chichicastenango Twelve," began the Mam Bible translation chain by recruiting Dorothy and Dudley Peck. The Pecks in turn helped train the Sywulkas, the Winters and the Scotchmers; the Winters trained Rubén Díaz; and the Mam translation work now goes on under Pedro Daniel Cabrera.

8

THE C.A.M. CATCHES THE VISION
FOR INDIAN WORK

In the 1970s, the Central American Mission changed its name to CAM International, for its missionaries were serving in Spain, Mexico, and Panama as well as in Central America. But the mission has changed more than its name and its geographical scope over the years. In this organization, perhaps more than in any other agency working in Guatemala, one can see the stormy transition from the position of "We shall have no Indian work separate from our Spanish work" to "Let us give the Indians God's Word in their own language."

A. Initial Chirripó Work.

The Central American Mission was founded on November 14, 1890, by Dr. C. I. Scofield of reference Bible fame. Its first missionaries, William and Minnie McConnell, reached Costa Rica in 1891. McConnell soon became burdened for the minority tribespeople of that country as well as for the Spanish-speaking majority. In answer to his prayers, Lewis Jamison and Henry Clay Dillon of the C.A.M. visited the Costa Rican Chirripó tribe in 1895, preaching through an interpreter. A year later, Jamison made a second trip into the tribe, and the number of baptized Chirripó believers reached thirty-two. But the government issued orders forbidding the missionary to return.

Meanwhile, Dillon had not only visited the Chirripó, but had also completed a survey of the Indian tribes of all Central

101

America. This study is known as the "Arthington Exploration" because it was financed by a dedicated Christian millionaire of Leeds, England, whose name was Robert Arthington.

Dillon's survey, which listed thirty-one tribes, led him to write: "It seems strange that such a great field lying just at our door with its many nations should have been absolutely neglected during the whole century of missions." He concluded that "no less than one hundred missionaries are needed to evangelize the Indians alone." (85)

Upon completing his survey, Dillon, a widower, returned briefly to Costa Rica and married C.A.M. missionary Margaret Neely. The two of them then moved to Guatemala, purposing to pioneer in Indian evangelism there, where the tribes were so much larger than those of Costa Rica. But within a short time, while on a trip to Honduras, he succumbed to a tropical fever. Although Dillon was not able to fulfill his dream of evangelizing Guatemala's Indians, he planted the seeds of vision for this work. Dr. Wilkins Winn has stated: "Dillon's untimely death in 1897 cut short his work which had a seminal impact on the Indian ministry of Protestant groups in Central America." (86)

The C.A.M.'s efforts among the Chirripó (Cabécar) Indians of Costa Rica was cut short when the government ordered Jamison to leave, and more than half a century passed before the work was resumed. By 1952, when Aziel and Marian Jones joined the C.A.M. and were assigned to the Chirripó people, the mission was fully backing the principle of Scripture translation into tribal languages. The Gospel of Mark was published in 1968, and other Scripture portions followed. In 1990 the Jones family (by then working independently of the C.A.M.) translated the last verse in Revelation and began the tedious process of revising and checking the entire New Testament for consistency in vocabulary. The New Testament was printed in Korea, brought to Costa Rica by ship, and dedicated with much rejoicing in October, 1993.

B. Cakchiquel Work.

Before his death, Dillon recruited Edward Bishop for missionary work. Bishop began his career in Honduras, but moved to Guatemala in 1899 and is considered the father and pioneer of C.A.M work in that country. (When Bishop arrived, the only other Protestant work in the country was the incipient Presbyterian ministry in Guatemala City and Quezaltenango.)

Mr. Bishop was a tireless evangelist and an excellent Bible teacher and church planter. Many of his first converts were Cakchiquel Indians, but he wished them to learn Spanish, read the Spanish Bible, and become a part of his Spanish-speaking churches. Other C.A.M. missionaries agreed with him. They saw no point in translating God's Word for illiterate people and echoed the opinion of one C.A.M. missionary who had said, "The few Indians who do read, read Spanish and can get the Gospel in that language."

The first members of the Central American Mission to learn and use an Indian language were the Cameron Townsends. Cameron, who had been a Bible colporteur before joining the C.A.M., had sold Quiché and Cakchiquel Scripture portions along with Spanish Bibles, but he found that the Indians could not understand the poorly translated Gospels any better than the Spanish Scriptures. So he set about to master the Cakchiquel tongue and translate the New Testament for this tribe. Since he had no prior training in linguistics, he struggled with Cakchiquel spelling, verbs, and sentence structure until an American archaeologist helped him realize that Mayan languages simply could not be forced into a classical Latin mold. After that, he progressed more rapidly in the translation, in spite of the fact that he did not have the opportunity to study linguistics at Harvard, as did the Pecks.

Townsend did not translate the New Testament entirely on his own. Not only did he have the valuable help of Cakchiquel co-translators such as Trinidad Bac and Joe Chicol, but he also consulted with Robinson and Burgess, as he had agreed to do at the 1921 Chichicastenango Conference. Although Robinson's death reduced the "Translation Committee" from three members to two, Townsend continued to value Burgess' input when they met together from time to time at Panajachel to go over the translation. Both Paul and Dora Burgess, on their part, also valued Townsend's input, and their letters show that they consulted him on the translation of difficult phrases, such as "the Son of Man." (In Mayan languages, when this phrase is translated literally, it would be understood by the average reader to refer either to Joseph or some other individual man, and thus would deny the Virgin birth. By translating whole ideas rather than making a literal word-for-word translation, Townsend solved this type of problem early in his translation, and was therefore able to help other missionaries who were not as far along as he.)

Townsend's tenacity and hard work paid off. His Cakchiquel translation, published by the American Bible Society in 1931, was the first complete New Testament to be published in a Guatemalan Indian tongue.

As we have noted in previous chapters, the Home Council of the Central American Mission was at first divided on the issue of whether or not missionaries should learn and use an Indian language. Some Council members, such as R. D. Smith, strongly opposed Townsend's efforts. But gradually, the Council as a whole came to see the value of reaching the Indians in their own tongue. In April 1925 the Council recognized Townsend as "Executive Secretary of the Cakchiquel Department."

The "Chichicastenango Twelve" played an important part in the gradual change of policy within the C.A.M. toward Indian work. Townsend and Robinson, of course, as members of this mission, made a significant impression on the Home Council both verbally and by the example of their success among the Indians. Dinwiddie and Legters, through their prayers and their persuasive letters, also helped to influence Luther Rees and other C.A.M. Council members, so that eventually the Council made a 180-degree turn, strongly supporting the separation of the Indian work from the Spanish, and giving its blessing to the ministry of Bible translation.

Townsend, as everyone knows, later moved on and teamed up with Legters to begin his own agency. But other C.A.M. missionaries followed in his steps, ministering to the Cakchiquel Indians. Some used the tribal dress and taught the people the Scriptures in their own language. Others, although never mastering the Cakchiquel tongue, have still given valuable service to this tribe.

Worthy of mention is the contribution of several C.A.M. single women to the Cakchiquel people: Irene Clifton, Naomi Gray, Lillian Jump, and Mildred Walkwitz. Other C.A.M. missionaries who have served the tribe include Archer Anderson, Paul Townsend, Albert Stradling, Floyd Nelson, Dr. H. A. Becker, Carl Malmstrom, Frank and Jenny Bundy, Ed and Ruth Read, Art and Marita Mikesell, the Ron Smiths, and the John Lohrenz family.

Joe Chicol, who assisted Cam with translation and who was also present at the first "Camp Wycliffe," revised Townsend's New Testament in 1950. Chicol's revision, for some reason, was apparently never very popular.

Later, Martha King of Wycliffe made a Cakchiquel translation which has been the basis for computer-produced simultaneous New Testaments in several Cakchiquel dialects. As of 1993, two of these had been printed and three more were nearing completion.

In the 1980s, some Cakchiquel believers gathered to see what could be done about getting the entire Bible in their language. As a result, CAM International is involved in Old Testament translation for this people group. The CAM translation consultants included Lillian Jump, John Lohrenz, and David and Helen Ekstrom. At this writing, the project, which is under the auspices of the United Bible Societies, is probably five or six years away from completion.

Cakchiquel evangelicals comprise one of the largest church groups among the Mayan tribes (including those in

Mexico). Nevertheless, some CAM missionaries believe that the churches would be even stronger if the Cakchiquel work were more clearly separated from the Spanish work. Because Townsend and the missionaries who came after him bowed to Mr. Bishop's feeling that to separate the Indian work from the Spanish would be like tearing warp and woof apart, the Cakchiquel congregations have not separated themselves from the Spanish-speaking churches in the same way in which the Mam, Quiché, and K'anjobal churches have done. Yet they continue to grow in numbers, even as does the church in Guatemala as a whole.

A tribe closely related to the Cakchiquel is the Tzutujil, found on the shores of Lake Atitlán. C.A.M. missionary Carl Moses encouraged national pastor Agustín Pop to translate Mark's Gospel for this tribe in 1955.

Wycliffe missionaries James and Judy Butler later translated the entire New Testament into Tzutujil. Unfortunately, the CAM-related churches have on the whole been unwilling to use that particular Tzutujil translation.

Pedro Samuc, a native Eastern Tzutujil speaker who graduated from CAM's seminary, was asked to make a new translation of the Scriptures for his tribe. In 1993, "after years of innumerable revisions and opposition," the Tzutujil New Testament for his people was printed and dedicated in a colorful ceremony.

Tzutujil CAM-related churches (as well as those of several other denominations) have grown steadily. In 1981, Juan José Ajú, pastor of the Santiago Atitlán congregation, reported that his church had grown to 1,400 members, and the other Tzutijil churches in the area also report steady conversions.

C. Pipil Work.

The first tribe to be evangelized by the C.A.M. may be said to be the Chirripó of Costa Rica; and the second, the Cakchiquel of Guatemala. Later the C.A.M. sought to spread the gospel among the Pipil (Nahuat) people, an ethnic minority in the tiny country of El Salvador.

Both Dinwiddie and Legters had a great burden for the Pipil Indians. As early as 1923, Dinwiddie enlisted five young women for this tribe, which numbered about 45,000 persons at that time. Only one of the young ladies, Miss Annie Esdon, eventually joined the C.A.M. However, the Home Council sent her, not to the Pipiles, but to the Cakchiquel field. It was fine for a young, single woman to be sent to help a married couple in an established work, such as Townsend had already raised up for the Cakchiquels. But it would not do to send her to a new field! The Council insisted that a man, not a woman, was needed for the Pipil tribe.

Dinwiddie, of course, was bitterly disappointed. He reminded the C.A.M. leaders that "possibly the strongest and most spiritual work among the Indians of the United States was undertaken by two women, the MacBeth sisters, among the Nez Perches [*sic*]." He was not in sympathy with the C.A.M.'s policy regarding women, and he wrote:

> Had we any intimation that this would be the attitude of the Mission, the five young ladies that applied to you for work in the Nahuat Tribe of Salvador, would not have taken this step. (8)

Later, Legters tried to persuade the C.A.M. to send to the Pipiles a linguistically gifted man who was born in Spain and raised in Puerto Rico. At that time, however, C.A.M. policy forbade their sending out Hispanics as full-fledged missionaries, relegating them to "native worker" status. (Fortunately, this policy has since been reversed.) The talented young Spaniard was not willing to go out with the lower salary and lesser status he would receive as a "native missionary." Once again, the desire of the Chichicastenango Twelve, that the Pipils be reached in their own language, was thwarted.

Another candidate suggested by Legters for the Pipil field—a Moody Bible Institute graduate doing home mission work in Wyoming—was disqualified because he was already thirty-eight years old. Still others were turned down by the C.A.M. because of their beliefs about baptism or speaking in tongues. Legters must have felt tempted to discouragement. Would he ever be able to find a suitable candidate for the Pipil field? Once he even confided to a friend that he wished Cameron Townsend could be split in two, so that half of him could be sent to El Salvador! Yet Legters did not give up. He told C.A.M.'s Acting Secretary Karl Hummel, "I shall continue to seek for the man."

It was not until 1927, after Dinwiddie's death, that a satisfactory candidate was found for the Nahuat tribe. Legters wrote to Karl Hummel:

> I have the support for two more missionaries, which I want, if possible, to send through your Board.... Will you please let me know the earliest date possible if MacNaughton [*sic*] could sail for Central America. I feel very confident that the thing to do is to put him in the territory of the Central American Mission among those Nahwat [*sic*] Indians. (88)

In December 1928, Mr. and Mrs. A. Roy MacNaught arrived in Sonsonate, El Salvador. Their support had been raised through efforts of L. L. Legters, and they had been prepared for tribal work by spending several months with the Townsends. When they settled among the Pipil people, however, they discovered that the Nahuat language was rapidly being displaced by Spanish.

The Pipil church grew steadily as the MacNaughts evangelized the area. Then came a severe setback in 1932 when "with astonishing suddenness and overwhelming tragedy, Satan wielded a master stroke, obliterating the effort of months." (89) Following an uprising, the Indian Christians were falsely labeled as Communists, and all the male believers who could be rounded up were shot. All the Bibles that could be found were burned, and the church building was totally cleaned out.

Mrs. MacNaught's failing health dealt a further blow to the Pipil work. Roy MacNaught was forced to go back to the

United States, where his wife passed away in 1933. Later, he returned to El Salvador, where with his second wife he devoted long years of service to its Spanish-speaking people.

By the 1950s, when the C.A.M. was ready to give serious thought to sending another missionary to translate the New Testament into the Pipil tongue, a survey conducted by Ed Sywulka revealed that the tribespeople had become so proficient in Spanish that they would not need a separate translation. Thus, the C.A.M. never gave a New Testament to this tribe which it had sought to evangelize. Nevertheless, the fact that this mission even began a work among the Pipil people was due largely to the initial surveys of Dinwiddie and Legters, to their constant urging that this tribe be reached, to their willingness to seek out recruits until they finally found one who was acceptable to the C.A.M.'s Home Council, and to Legters' successful efforts in raising the money for his passage and support.

D. "Del Norte" Work.

By late 1927, the Central American Mission was so enthusiastic about Indian work that their December 19 minutes read:

> Moved and carried that a favorable reply be sent to Mr. L. L. Legters, Field Secretary of the Pioneer Mission Agency, as to his proposition that the C.A.M. undertake work among the Indians in Southern Mexico, it being understood that such work shall be contiguous to our work in Guatemala and that men and means be provided apart from our present organization and finances, and also that our entrance be subject to agreement with the Presbyterians. (90)

Although the desire to enter Chiapas was strong, men and money were in short supply. Consequently, the Central American Mission did not send missionaries to Mexico at that time. It remained for Wycliffe translators to reach the Tzeltal, Tzotzil and Chol tribes nearly two decades later.

There was a man, however, for the "Del Norte" Indians of Guatemala. And there was money for the new missionary and his wife, thanks to the Pioneer Mission Agency. Newberry and Kitty Cox were recruited by L. L. Legters for this "tribe" (later they discovered that it was a whole cluster of tribes!) and they applied to the Central American Mission for Indian work. Legters secured $400 for their travel expenses, $100 for their outfit, and arranged for a Mr. M. B. Lane to assume their monthly support.

The Coxes, small in stature but large in heart and vision, sailed to Guatemala in October 1928. In 1931 they opened up work in San Miguel Acatán in the province of Huehuetenango. "With their eyes on the double goal of preaching the gospel to every creature and giving the 40,000 Conobs the New Testament in their own tongue, this gifted, prepared couple" lived among the Indians for nearly thirty years. (91) The Gospels of John and Mark in Conob (K'anjobal) were published first, and in 1953 the entire Conob New Testament was turned over to the American Bible Society for publication. It was dedicated in 1955, and a hymnal and primers were also published.

The Chuj and Jacaltec tribes are also part of the "Del Norte" group which the Coxes sought to reach with the Gospel. C.A.M. work among these people has been carried out primarily by David and Helen Ekstrom.

David Ekstrom, like his wife, is a second generation missionary. Both Oliver Ekstrom (David's father) and Newberry Cox (David's senior missionary) were influenced by Legters. In fact, it was Cox, a Legters recruit, who in turn recruited David Ekstrom for work among the Indians. Thus we see the influence of "The Chichicastenango Twelve" extending to more than one missionary generation.

David and Helen established residence in San Sebastián Coatán in 1953, with the purpose of translating the Bible for the Chuj tribe. Their "translation plus general missionary work" record since that time has been phenomenal. Because they belong to CAM International, they are permitted to engage directly in church planting, something they could not do had they gone out under Wycliffe Bible Translators.

While devoting much time to church duties, they have also done more actual translation than many full-time translators.

The Ekstroms' translations of the Scriptures into the Chuj, K'anjobal, and Jacaltec languages have contributed greatly to the numerical and spiritual growth of the church among these people groups. Their ministry of evangelism and teaching has been no less effective.

The New Testament in San Mateo Chuj was published in 1970, after fourteen years of painstaking effort on the part of David and Helen Ekstrom and their Indian co-translators. Wycliffe translator Kenneth Williams, working in another Chuj dialect, aided them with valuable insights.

After the original Cox K'anjobal New Testament had gone through three reprintings, David and Helen Ekstrom began a revision (actually a re-translation) of this work. The revised K'anjobal New Testament was published in 1973.

The Ekstroms also translated a Jacaltec New Testament, which was published in 1979. Jacaltec Old Testament translation is yet another part of this couple's continuing linguistic endeavors. Together with their co-worker Gregorio Montejo, the Ekstroms have recently worked on a revision of the book of Proverbs in Jacaltec.

In 1980 the Ekstroms began the momentous task of translating the entire K'anjobal Old Testament. The complete Bible in K'anjobal was dedicated with joyful praise in 1989, just fifty years after Newberry and Kitty Cox began the New Testament translation in this language.

A second Chuj New Testament, translated by David and Helen, was printed in Korea and scheduled for distribution in Guatemala by mid-April 1994. The Ekstroms also organized a distribution program designed to get copies of the New Testament into churches and schools where the Chuj language is spoken, and to distribute cassette recordings of the K'anjobal and Chuj Scriptures to people who are unable to read.

In addition to their own translation efforts, David and Helen Ekstrom have assisted other translators and typed manuscripts for them, prepared hymnbooks for several tribes, taught missionary children, established a Bible Institute and a radio station for the K'anjobal people, and engaged in evangelism, church planting, and Bible school teaching.

Church growth among the "Del Norte" tribal groups has been prodigious. In some Chuj and K'anjobal areas, more than half of the population is evangelical. Due to political and economic turmoil in Guatemala, the 1980s saw an exodus of K'anjobal people. While the uprooting of an ethnic minority is never without its problems, it has opened new doors of opportunity for CAM International. Jim and Gail McKelvey of CAM are ministering to a large group of K'anjobales—counted in the thousands—who have resettled in Southern California. And they are reaching these Indians in their own language!

E. Mam Work.

Early in Guatemalan mission history, the large Mam field was divided between the Presbyterians and the Central American Mission, a division which is still loosely held today.

Herbert and Mary Toms, two of the original "Chichicastenango Twelve," were burdened for the Mam Indians in the C.A.M. territory. After the 1921 conference, Dinwiddie began sending money (through Robinson, the L.A.I.M. treasurer) for the support of a Mam evangelist named Esteban. Later, after Bishop reprimanded Dinwiddie for sending funds to the field without going through proper channels, he remitted the money through the Central American Mission, for he was eager to maintain good relations with this agency.

Dinwiddie wrote a long letter to Luther Rees, chairman of the C.A.M. He wanted to send his Pioneer Mission Agency recruits out under the Central American Mission, but he wanted to make sure that they would be allowed to do the Indian work for which they were applying:

> These volunteers for Indian service would not apply to you for promiscuous service under your Mission but primarily for the Indians. (92)

Dinwiddie also wanted to make sure that his recruits

would be allowed to translate the Bible for the Indians. He cited the work of the Moravians in Nicaragua and that of the Bolivian Indian Mission among the Quechuas. Their success, Dinwiddie believed, was due to the fact that they were using the native languages and giving the tribespeople God's Word in their own tongue. Then he gave another example, one from Rees' own agency. Toms among the Mams was *not* using the Indian language himself. Townsend among the Cakchiquel people *was* using the language and translating the Bible.

> The comparison of results *among the Indians* obtained by Townsend and by the Toms (presented in the *Central American Bulletin* of July 12, 1922, on pages 9 and 10) afford most striking evidences of the relative effectiveness of direct and indirect language work. The Spanish work of the Toms is splendid, but when you consider that their territory is variously reckoned to be from 75% to 90% Indian in population their results in their meagerness are pitiably pathetic in comparison with Townsend's. (93)

Luther Rees read Dinwiddie's letter carefully, but he was unwilling to concede that the Cakchiquel success was due to Townsend's use of the Indian language. He wrote back:

> In comparing the Indian work of Mr. Toms with that of Mr. Townsend, it should be borne in mind that although Mr. Townsend has been on the field only a short time, he stepped into a field where Mr. Bishop and his native evangelists, including Indian evangelists, have been laboring for many years. (94)

By 1922, as we have noted, Herbert Toms' enthusiasm for the Indian work seemed to have waned, and by 1925 the young couple resigned from the Central American Mission. Dinwiddie in 1922 could not have known that it would be more than a decade before a missionary translator and linguist for the Mams would be sent out by the Central American Mission.

After Dinwiddie's death, Legters carried on his concern for the Mams. Through the Pioneer Mission Agency, he helped to raise support for Bessie Cushnie, who first worked with the Coxes and later became the second Mrs. Oliver Ekstrom. In

1933 Oliver and Bessie Ekstrom settled in San Pedro Sacatepé-quez, a highland city in the Mam area of San Marcos Province. For two years they applied themselves tirelessly to evangelism. But their work was cut short in 1935 when Mr. Ekstrom contracted typhus while on a trip. Within a short time, he was in the Lord's presence.

Meanwhile, God had prepared a curly-haired "missionary kid" from Africa for a lifetime of service to the Mams. In 1929, young Ed Sywulka yielded his life to Christ at a Keswick conference. Later, as a student at Columbia Bible College, Ed heard Legters talk about his survey trips through Mexico, Central America, and South America. When Sywulka told Legters that he felt called to tribal work, the older man counseled him, "Ed, go somewhere where there are Indians!" By this, he meant that Ed should go to the large groups of Guatemala or Mexico rather than to the small tribes along the Amazon. In this way, Ed was steered into applying to the C.A.M.

Sywulka graduated from college in 1932, and in 1934 Townsend picked him up in South Carolina and took him to Arkansas as the very first student at the initial "Camp Wycliffe." Here the young recruit absorbed Townsend's Cakchiquel grammar classes, Joe Chicol's lessons in Cakchiquel pronunciation, and Legters' messages on the Victorious Life.

By the end of August, Ed and three other young men left Arkansas in order to take a two-weeks' course in phonetics from Dr. McCreery of Biola in Los Angeles. Due to his wife's illness, Townsend was unable to accompany the recruits. But with his characteristic generosity, he loaned his car to the students for their trip.

In October of that year, with their Camp Wycliffe experiences still fresh in their minds, Sywulka and Chicol set out together for Guatemala by train. The financial support of both was provided by Legters himself.

Legters assumed that both young men would join Cameron Townsend in the Cakchiquel field. But the Pecks invited Ed to work among the Mams, and the C.A.M. leaders were in agreement. They informed Legters: "The *urgent* need of the C.A.M. is the work in the Mam District from San Marcos... Brother Sywulka would be quite willing to take up that work." (95)

Legters' answer shows how important the *Indian* work was to him:

> By this mail I received a letter from Joe Chicol also. My hands are entirely off the matter. The only thing that I ask is that they do Indian work wherever the Lord leads them. Far be it from me to try in any way to dictate in the faintest way. If the Lord opens the Mam work for Sywulka I am perfectly agreed, if among any of the other Indians, I am perfectly agreed ... By all means assure them that any way or place the Lord leads him is agreeable to me, just so they do not switch him to Ladino work. As to Joe Chicol, I think the natural thing would be that he work in the language he understands... I am sending him $15.00 per month with the thought that he and Edward were together, since he is not I shall send a little more.(96)

So Sywulka was sent to the Mams. The Pecks convinced him that the only way to learn the language was to live among the people, so he took up residence on the platform of a small chapel near Ostuncalco, bought a rude chair in the market, made a bed out of planks, and ate his meals in a Mam home.

A few months later, the Pecks asked Sywulka to help them with the last stages of their New Testament translation. Then, while they took a furlough, he helped with the final corrections and proofreading.

In 1938 Sywulka married Pauline Burgess, a daughter of "Chichicastenango Twelve" members Paul and Dora Burgess. Later the young couple moved to Huehuetenango Province and completed a Mam New Testament in that dialect. The first edition was dedicated in 1969. A second edition, slightly revised, was printed in 1975 and a third edition appeared in 1979.

Some thirty years after the Pecks' New Testament was completed, Sywulka began to revise their work for the Ostuncalco Mams. This revision, begun in 1970 and completed in 1973, may more properly be considered a new translation. This work has gone through two printings in order to satisfy the demand.

Trailblazers for Translators

In 1974 Ed Sywulka took on the challenge of translating the Old Testament into Mam. He had earlier translated some Old Testament portions for Sunday school lessons, but found the Hebrew imagery to be obscure and difficult. With this in view, he returned to school. At an age when many men begin retirement, Ed Sywulka enrolled in Dallas Seminary to study Hebrew. In 1983 the published "Abbreviated Old Testament" consisting of selected Scripture portions in Mam was dedicated. By 1988 Sywulka and his Mam co-workers had completed the translation of the entire Mam Old Testament, and the process of checking and getting it ready for the presses had begun.

In November 1993, four thousand believers gathered in San Sebastián Huehuetenango to dedicate the newly printed entire Mam Bible. Later, similar dedication services were celebrated in other Mam towns.

When Sywulka began his lifework, there were fewer than sixty Mam Indian believers in the C.A.M. field (in the provinces of Huehuetenango and San Marcos). Fifty years later, the CAM-related Mam Evangelical Council (similar to a presbytery or a conference of churches) included a Christian community of 28,000 persons. By 1994 there were 140 CAM-related Mam churches and congregatons.

The Mam believers have not only the Old and New Testaments, but their own Sunday school lesson series, a hymnbook, and a full-color Bible story book prepared by Pauline Sywulka. The Ezra Bible Institute serves the Mam people in four centers, *Radio Buenas Nuevas* broadcasts in Mam and four other Indian languages, the Mams have organized their own Mayan Missionary Society, and the ECCO publishing house is producing new literature for the Christians.

CAM missionaries who—along with the Sywulkas— have contributed to the Mam work include: Wayne and Kitty Gute, Marge Hutchins, John Beverage, several nurses, and Mike Stephenson.

Wycliffe missionaries have also joined the Mam translation efforts, some helping Ed Sywulka with the Old Testament, and others working on new translations into regional Mam dialects. Still other members of Wycliffe have translated Scripture into closely related languages found within the area served by CAM.

Notable among these are Harry and Lucille McArthur, whose translation of the New Testament into Aguacatec greatly increased the membership of the CAM-related Aguacatec church. In November 1993, at the very time the entire Mam Bible was dedicated, the Aguacatec tribe was celebrating the arrival of their revised New Testament with Psalms, produced by the McArthurs and their dedicated co-translators.

The church growth, the translations, and the literature work among the Mams both in the Presbyterian field and the C.A.M. field can be traced back directly to the vision of the "Chichicastenango Twelve." For it was Dinwiddie who recruited the Pecks for the Presbyterian field. And it was Legters who recruited Sywulka for the Mams in the C.A.M. field and who provided his support. Ed Sywulka also acknowledges his debt to three other members of the "Chichicastenango Twelve"— Cameron Townsend, who trained him in linguistics, and Paul and Dora Burgess, who brought up and trained his wife!

Thus the Central American Mission, whose field leaders and Home Council members once strongly opposed the idea of using the Indian tongues, of translating the Bible for the tribes, and of separating the Indian churches from the Spanish, completely changed its policies, pioneered in Bible translation, and continues to encourage distinctive work for the tribes. CAM-related churches among the Cakchiquel, Mam, K'anjobal, Chuj, Aguacatec, Jacaltec, Tzutujil, and Quiché tribes are a tribute to the vision of this agency's leadership and to the diligence of its missionaries and national workers. They are also a tribute to the prayers of Dinwiddie, and to the untiring recruitment and training efforts of Legters and Townsend—three outstanding members of the "Chichicastenango Twelve."

9

OTHER MISSION AGENCIES IN GUATEMALA CATCH THE VISION

A. The Primitive Methodists

1.) Initial work. The Primitive Methodist Church, a small denomination concentrated mainly in the eastern U.S.A., entered Guatemala in 1922. The first missionary couple they sponsored were Truman and Carrie Furman, who had previously worked in that country as Pentecostal missionaries.

The second Primitive Methodist missionary was Amos Bradley, sent to Totonicapán to take over the work of Pentecostal missionaries Mr. and Mrs. Albert Hines, who were returning to Texas. With his broad hat and weather-beaten face, Bradley looked more like a farmer than a missionary, but he had a heart for evangelism.

As soon as Paul Burgess heard that the Primitive Methodists were buying the Hines' property and sending a missionary to Totonicapán, he wrote to his friend Legters: "We must convince them to use the Quiché language."

Convince them he did! So much so, that Amos Bradley set to work, not only to learn Quiché, but also to help translate John's Gospel into that tongue. Burgess reported to Townsend in 1923:

> We are working away on Quiché and tho the other things seem to crowd in constantly, are surely making some little progress tho it is often not visible. Mr. Bradley of Totonicapán is also getting interested and we are having some conferences of his workers with our

118

own to get as representative variations of the languages as possible together, so as to find expressions that will be clear to all. (97)

As has been noted, the first edition of John's Gospel was partially financed by a supporter whom L. L. Legters had recruited; the Primitive Methodists as a group did not help with the cost. By 1927, however, the Primitive Methodist Board was so enthusiastic about Bible translation that they helped finance the publication of Matthew's Gospel in Quiché that year.

In 1928 the Bradleys took over the Chichicastenango mission station. Thus the work begun by Dr. Secord (a Brethren missionary), and transferred to the Treichlers of the Central American Mission for a brief time in the early 1920s, became Primitive Methodist in 1928. Although the Bradleys left two years later because of family and financial problems, the Evangelical Church in Chichicastenango has remained largely Primitive Methodist to this day.

2. *Further work.* Many Primitive Methodist missionaries have made valuable contributions to the work among the Quiché Indians. An example of their service may be seen in one couple, William and Margaret Hays, who gave four decades of service to the Quiché people.

In early 1939, while Bill Hays was a senior at Wheaton College, L. L. Legters addressed the student body, emphasizing that the doors in Guatemala were wide open to the preaching of the gospel and that the percentage of Indians in that country was higher than in any other Central or South American republic.

As a result of Legters' impassioned plea for laborers, reinforced by contacts with furloughing Presbyterian and Primitive Methodist missionaries, Hays and his bride applied to the Primitive Methodist Board, were accepted, and sailed to Guatemala in October of 1939. Within a few months they were settled in Chichicastenango, learning Spanish and attempting to learn Quiché. Although they never attained proficiency in Quiché, their forty years of dedication to Quiché church planting and

evangelism, as well as to Bible Institute teaching and administration, are representative of the labors of many other Primitive
Methodist missionaries who have served Christ and the Quiché
people in Guatemala. Among these we may name Harold Bar-
rett, Harry Granger, Loren and Helen Anderson, and Grace
Kenney Par.

The vision born in Chichicastenango at the Indian Conference blossomed and bore fruit in that very city nearly two decades later. For it was Leonard Legters, stirred by God's Spirit
in Chichicastenango in 1921, who recruited Hays for long-term
service in that community and its surrounding territory.

The Primitive Methodists later took up work in the Ixil
tribe as well as in the Quiché tribe, but the translation was left
to cooperating Wycliffe missionaries—Ray and Helen Elliott—
rather than to their own staff.

B. THE FRIENDS MISSION

1. Initial work. The work of the Friends in Guatemala began after two men, Thomas Kelly and Clark Buckley, heard
Edward Bishop speak in Bakersfield, California, on the subject
of Guatemala's great need.

After obtaining a ton of Bibles and Scripture portions, the
two men left California on January 2, 1902. By July of that
year they had initiated their work in Chiquimula, in eastern
Guatemala.

From the beginning, these pioneers had a burden for reaching the Indians of that area. Their church and educational ministries soon expanded, and new Friends recruits joined their
ranks. Missionary superintendent Esther Smith was used of the
Lord in a revival which swelled the ranks of the Chiquimula
Church to nearly a thousand adult believers in 1918.

2. Further work. In 1921 and 1922, Dinwiddie and Legters
traveled to Chiquimula to preach the Victorious Christian Life
in that area, as well as to survey the tribal needs. They reported, however, that nearly all the Indians around Chiquimula had
mastered Spanish and were no longer using their native tongue.

Thus, while they urged missionary Esther Smith to send her "native workers" to the L.A.I.M. conferences, their concern for the Indians of eastern Guatemala was primarily for evangelism and spiritual growth rather than for Bible translation. Nevertheless, small pockets of Indians within the area served by the Friends Mission continue to use tribal languages, and Friends missionaries have contributed to Scripture translation. In 1949, the American Bible Society, the Guatemalan Ministry of Education, and the Friends Mission cooperated in establishing an official Chortí alphabet. Friends missionary Helen Oakley, previously assigned to Chiquimula, had moved to Jocotán with the purpose of reaching the Chortí people. She translated hymns, Bible portions, and Mark's Gospel, which was published in 1958. Her fellow-missionaries, John and Joyce McNichols, translated portions of the Life of Christ, some Old Testament stories, and the book of Acts, which appeared in 1970. Further Chortí translation is being carried out by Wycliffe missionaries John and Diana Lubeck.

C. THE NAZARENE MISSION

1) Initial work. The Nazarenes are considered to be the fourth missionary agency to enter Guatemala (after the Presbyterian, Central American, and Friends Missions). The date of their arrival in Guatemala is officially given as 1904, but in reality their work, like that of the Primitive Methodists, was based on an earlier Pentecostal effort.

The tribes falling within the Nazarene field are the Kekchí, the Pocomchí, the Carib, the Mopán, and the Rabinal-Achí. For nearly forty years, however, the Nazarene missionaries attempted to reach these peoples through Spanish with minimal success.

2) Further work. The man who gave the vision for Bible translation to the Nazarenes in Guatemala was William Sedat. Like so many other translators, he was strongly influenced by the giants of the "Chichicastenango Twelve." Along with Ken

Pike, Max Lathrop, Brainerd Legters and Richmond McKinney, he attended the second session of "Camp Wycliffe" in 1935 and studied under Townsend, Legters, Chicol and McCreery.

Sponsored by the Pioneer Mission Agency, Sedat went to Guatemala and began his work of translation among the Kekchí people. L. L. Legters had once again arranged for a young translator's support to be provided. Legters wanted his young protégé to belong to an established missionary agency; he tried to persuade the leaders of the Central American Mission to take the fledgling under their wings as an associate.

Before this could be arranged, however, Bill Sedat found a bride—Betty Rusling, whom he married in 1940—and joined the Nazarene Mission. When Bill and Betty's translation ministry began to result in church growth, leaders of the Nazarene board saw the importance of reaching people for Christ in their own tongues.

In 1961, after more than twenty years of learning Kekchí, reducing it to writing, and translating God's Word, the Sedats saw the fruit of their labors —the published New Testament. After Bill Sedat's death in 1971, his wife continued to do further linguistic work, translating the New Testament into Pocomchí. More recently, Wycliffe missionaries Francis Eachus and Ruth Carlson translated and published Old Testament portions and revised the translation of the Kekchí New Testament. Over 1,500 Christians gathered joyously in Cobán to dedicate these published Scriptures in 1984. Even greater was the rejoicing in 1990 when the entire Bible in Kekchí rolled off the presses and was placed in the hands of the people.

Milton Coke describes the Kekchí evangelical explosion thus:

A peoples movement is sweeping so many Kekchí into the churches that pastors can no longer keep track of the growth ... Tremendous church growth since 1965 has attracted Southern Baptists, Mennonites and Assemblies of God missionaries. Fran and Ruth have helped them to learn Kekchí and along with the Sedats helped reverse the Protestant emphasis on Spanish ministry. The Kekchí hymnbook and New Testament are widely used, and...Roman Catholics are encouraged now to read the Scriptures. (98)

E. GENERAL CONCLUSIONS

The influence of the "Chichicastenango Twelve" can be felt in all the missionary agencies who pioneered in Guatemala. It was those men of vision—Dinwiddie, Legters, Burgess and Townsend—who began reversing "the Protestant empahsis on Spanish ministry," and it was their recruits—missionaries like the Pecks, the Sywulkas, the Sedats, and the Hays—who continued to spread the vision.

The results of this emphasis are clearly seen in the tremendous church growth which Guatemala has experienced in recent years; some figures state that as much as one fourth of the total population is evangelical. Among the ethnic minorities, this church growth can be attributed not only to a great working of the Spirit of God, but also to the faithfulness of men and women who have made the Word of God available to people in their own tongues.

Why did the L.A.I.M. not survive for long as a separate organization? One answer is: A separate organization was no longer needed, because the mission agencies were themselves catching the vision. Paul Burgess expressed it succinctly in his Diamond Jubilee History of Evangelical Work in Guatemala:

> Cameron Townsend and Elbert Robinson came from the USA, commissioned by the Central American Mission.... They set themselves to learn Cakchiquel, they began to experiment with translation, and they established a small Institute to train Indian workers. Some of the missionaries sympathized with their effort and others condemned it, so that both the Central American Mission and the Presbyterian Mission were at the point of splitting over this issue. The issue was further complicated by the arrival of Mr. Dinwiddie and Mr. Legters, who had the vision of organizing a new mission for Indians, separate from those already established.
>
> It would take a long time to trace the story of the struggles over the Indian work, but the results can be clearly seen. The missions, little by little, grew to understand the usefulness of this type of work and began to support it, so that it was no longer necessary for a separate agency to carry it out.(99)

10

THE LEGACY OF THE
CHICHICASTENANGO TWELVE

God was at work in a mighty way in January 1921, when twelve men and women met for prayer and planning in Chichicastenango. Their gathering may be compared to the famed Haystack Prayer Meeting at Williams College more than one hundred years before. Both gatherings were characterized by prayer, both were landmarks in the history of mission advance, and both resulted in God's doing something new. The Haystack Prayer Meeting was the birthplace of American foreign missions; the Chichicastenango conference was the birthplace of a united effort to reach the tribes and give them God's Word in their own languages—an effort which not only changed the policies of existing mission societies, but which also resulted in the formation of the L.A.I.M. and the Pioneer Mission Agency, forebears of the Wycliffe Bible Translators.

Among the twelve persons who gathered at Chichicastenango and prayed until midnight for the tribes, then shouted "Hallelujah, it is time for Jehovah to work!" were a few whose enthusiasm shortly waned. But there were others whose vision grew more bold and clear as time went on. These may be considered the giants of that conference: Howard Dinwiddie, Leonard Legters, Paul and Dora Burgess, Cameron Townsend and W. E. Robinson.

Much has been said about Townsend's influence on the modern missionary movement. Because of his vision, perseverance and leadership qualities, hundreds of minority ethnic groups throughout the whole world now have God's Word in their own tongue. Thousands of modern translators were either recruited by him, taught by him, or inspired by his example and his encouragement. He lived the longest, traveled the most widely, and is by far the best-known of the "Chichicastenango Twelve."

Perhaps not enough has been said about the other men and women who prayed the same prayers and dreamed the same dreams in the early 1920s. Some, like Robinson and Dinwiddie, did not live to see those dreams materialize; but their early death should not detract from the influence of their vision and faith. They, too, left a legacy for the tribes.

And what of the influence of Paul and Dora Burgess? Because they stuck with one tribe and one mission board for over forty years, they were never as widely known as are men and women who travel much and establish new agencies. Yet they too left a legacy for those who followed them in tribal work. Dora Burgess translated the Quiché New Testament, and Paul influenced his own board as well as the Primitive Methodists and others to use the vernacular Indian tongue. He encouraged Townsend by supporting his ideas and aiding him with the Cakchiquel translation; and he helped Legters initiate the long series of survey trips which resulted in the recruitment of hundreds of new missionaries for the tribes.

Rev. Howard Dinwiddie also left a legacy. He was a spiritual giant who envisioned a global effort to give the Scriptures to tribal peoples. He was tireless in prayer, in travel, in recruitment efforts, in raising funds for national workers, and in organizing new agencies for pioneer work.

Between 1921 and 1925, he made six trips to Latin America for ministry and exploration. One of these was a 3,000-mile journey through the Amazon jungle.

He literally had the whole world on his heart, for he was burdened for Africa and Asia as well as for the Indians of Latin America. He traveled from Philadelphia to Chicago, to California and to the British Isles to speak on the Victorious Christian Life and to raise recruits, financial support, and prayer partners for the world's unreached minorities.

His seventh and last exploratory trip was to the Arakan Hills of Assam in northeast India. Together with A. I. Garrison of the Christian and Missionary Alliance, he had visited several mission stations and was planning to survey the unexplored regions of northeast India. In the Lushai hills district, he died suddenly of typhoid fever on December 27, 1925, at forty-eight years of age.

Fittingly, his body was laid to rest there in India, where the first revival flames of the Victorious Life Movement were sparked. When Mr. and Mrs. Borton of the Victorious Life Testimony received the cable and sought to break the news to Mrs. Dinwiddie and her eleven-year-old son, they found that God had already prepared her. She knew inwardly that her husband was with God.

A memorial folder prepared by The Victorious Life Testimony, the Pioneer Mission Agency, and America's Keswick stated:

> His vision of the mission fields of the world and of the untouched regions was almost unique in our generation. His pioneer work in Central and South America is in no small measure responsible for the present interest and activity in the Christian Church in behalf of the long neglected American Indians. It was largely his conviction of the need of some organized agency to ascertain the needs in the unreached fields and to undertake the supply of missionaries and funds to the organized mission boards for occupation, that led to the formation of the Pioneer Mission Agency. Through him many lives in the homeland have been touched into a realization of their all-victorious Savior and Lord and of their responsibility for carrying His Gospel to those who know Him not.... Will you not pray that God may clearly indicate the leader upon whose shoulders Mr. Dinwiddie's mantle should fall, and under whose direction the pioneer missionary work in the untouched regions of the world may go forward? (100)

The mantle fell quite naturally upon the shoulders of Leonard L. Legters. He continued making exploratory trips almost annually, carrying on a Victorious Christian Life conference ministry in the United States and other countries. For nineteen consecutive years he served as Field Secretary of the Pioneer Mission Agency, raising up men and money for the unreached tribes and working to persuade mission board leaders of "the necessity of translating the Bible" into Indian languages. (101)

Some of his recruits were most unlikely candidates. For instance, there was Miss Ella Bennet. A forty-year-old graduate of the Bible Institute of Los Angeles, no mission board would take her because of her age. But inspired by Legters, she went out independently to Guatemala in 1924, worked with the Burgesses, and preached in both Spanish and Quiché to all who would come and sit on her porch.

In 1926 and 1927 Legters conducted two extensive surveys along the Amazon. His son David Brainerd, a seventeen-year-old, accompanied him on the journey up the Xingu River and its tributaries. Later, speaking dramatically and impellingly, Legters used the survey information to challenge scores of young people in the United States to volunteer for missionary service among the Indians of Latin America. When Townsend, still laboring in Guatemala, saw Legters' pictures of the Indians along the Xingu, his heart became more burdened than ever for the unreached tribes beyond Guatemala's borders.

When Legters returned from his Xingu trip, he found that his wife, who had never been well enough to accompany him on his trips, was more seriously ill than ever before. It was not long before the cancer which she had been battling took her life. Thus Leonard lost both his closest associate—Howard Dinwiddie—and his devoted wife within a short time.

Later, back at Keswick in New Jersey, Legters met a spirited college professor named Edna Hafer who shared his interest in the unreached tribes. They were married September 9, 1931, in Chambersburg, Pennsylvania.

It was also in 1931 that Legters, together with Dr. James G. Dale, visited the Aztec Indians at Tamazunchale, Mexico.

The two men climbed a hill and then dropped to their knees, claiming the site as a future mission station and Bible training school for Indians. Thus was born the Mexican Indian Mission (now part of the Unevangelized Fields Mission), designed to reach the more than a half million Aztecs of Central Mexico. Less than three years later, Dr. Dale's son John joined his parents and began learning Aztec for the purpose of translating the New Testament into that tongue.

The year 1931 also marked the publication and dedication of the Cakchiquel New Testament in Guatemala. This news, of course, brought great joy to Leonard Legters, but it was followed by sadness the following year when he learned that Cameron Townsend had been ordered back to California to recover from tuberculosis.

Townsend's illness in no way constricted the scope of his vision. He was still dreaming of reaching tribes far beyond Guatemala's borders, of penetrating the jungles along the Xingu by plane, of translating God's Word for the many hidden peoples which Legters and Dinwiddie had discovered.

The C.A.M. leadership was aware of Townsend's dreams. They struggled with the issue of expansion, and even considered a merger which would have enlarged their borders. But in the end they decided they were not ready to expand their work to the extent that Townsend envisioned. He would have to launch out on his own. Aziel Jones has written:

> The Council ... members struggled to stretch their imaginations to match the vision of Cameron Townsend. After fifteen years of pursuing a vision which perhaps was beyond the scope of his Mission ... Townsend resigned from the CAM. Shortly before his resignation, there was a discussion of a merger of the The Central American Mission, Inland South American Union, and the Orinoco River Mission. This meant a field which would reach from Chiapas, Mexico to Amazonia. Late in 1932, therefore, the Executive Committee, thinking of the possible merger and of Townsend's visions, authorized Mr. Malmstrom to inform him of this. But the merger never materialized and Cameron Townsend went on to found the Wycliffe Bible Translators.(102)

In late 1932, Legters received a letter from the Townsends with some amazing news. Cameron and Elvira had definitely left the Cakchiquels, they said, and would be available to begin a new pioneer work in South America as soon as God restored their health.

Legters felt that he needed to talk this possibility over with Cameron in person, rather than merely by mail. His surveys had led him to feel strongly that the Townsends could do more good in Mexico, where the tribes were larger and more accessible. So Leonard and Edna set out for California, where they were able to visit the Townsends in Santa Ana in February, 1933.

Once again the two men discussed a strategy for reaching Bibleless tribes, just as they had done in Chichicastenango and San Antonio twelve years earlier. Legters' surveys led him to advise Townsend to begin a new translation ministry in Mexico, where there were an estimated fifty large tribes without the Bible, rather than to start over again in South America, where the tribes were much smaller. Legters spoke of the work which the Dales had begun, and he shared his burden for the large Mayan tribe in Yucatán, as yet without the Scriptures in their own tongue.

Townsend listened to Legters describe the needs in Mexico, and then he shared his own burden. He had a clear vision of the need for a training camp to teach young volunteers from all mission agencies both the basics of "how to rough it" on the mission field and the linguistic principles which would enable them to translate God's Word into an unwritten language.

As the two friends shared their common burdens, Townsend agreed to begin a new ministry in Mexico, and Legters agreed to cooperate in establishing a summer training camp. At that time, apparently, they had no particular thought of spawning a new mission sending society. It was understood that this camp should be an extension of the Pioneer Mission Agency, and that it should serve to train the recruits which the P.M.A.

was raising up, helping to support financially, and sending out under other societies.

After Legters left, Townsend immediately began to make notes for the lectures he planned to give on "methods of reaching Indians," for the training camp was scheduled to begin in the summer of 1934.

Meanwhile, the work of the Pioneer Mission Agency and the Indian Mission Committee of America had been going forward, in spite of the Great Depression which had drastically reduced donations. Dr. Thomas Moffett, Secretary of the Indian Mission Committee, wrote to Paul Burgess:

> The balance available for Marcelino's salary is very small, I learn. What provision you and Mr. Legters have in mind for his further support I have not heard. May his great labor of love and devotion be richly rewarded!
>
> Cameron Townsend is nearby at Santa Ana, and according to recent reports is making improvement in health.
>
> How little our Mission organizations have been able to undertake and to accomplish for the Indians! Alcibaides Iglesias has recently gone to his own tribe, the San Blas in Panama. We are keeping up the Mexico City Indian work for the Federal Trade School pupils, and maintain a library-reading room. But funds are scant during these distressing days of insecurities. (103)

L. L. Legters had been concerned for the San Blas Indians for several years, and had been trying to get the Central American Mission to enter that tribe. Although the C.A.M.'s Karl Hummel wrote him that they "would be very happy to undertake the San Blas Indian work, provided men and means are raised up" (104), the C.A.M. was never able to follow through with this desire. Not only were men and means lacking, but the Panama government forbade foreigners to enter the San Blas territory. Therefore it remained for Iglesias, a San Blas Indian who graduated from Bible school in Nyack, New York, to reach his own people. Thanks to the Pioneer Mission Agency and the Indian Mission of America, he went out backed by the financial and prayer support of God's people.

Even while Legters continued to raise up recruits and finances for the tribes of Central America, his burden for Mexico's Indians deepened. In August 1933 he returned to Keswick Bible Conference in New Jersey where he shared the platform with Dr. Dale.

Dr. Dale told how the Mexican government had restricted the activities of established foreign missionaries and refused entry permits to new missionaries. He then challenged the conference delegates to pray for Mexico's Indians.

God moved in a mighty way at that gathering, just as He had in Chichicastenango in 1921. Leonard and Edna Legters spent all night in prayer in the auditorium, and the next day Addison Raws, Keswick's director, announced that while meals would be served as usual for anyone who wished to eat, he and the other leaders were planning to give themselves to prayer and fasting on behalf of Mexico's tribes.

After the announcement, the waitresses went to the dining room, set food on the tables, and rang the dinner bell. When not a single person appeared to partake of the meal, the waitresses gathered up the food and joined the small groups who were asking God to open Mexico's doors. Later they learned that a group at the original Keswick Conference in England was praying for Mexico at the very same time!

Legters described the day thus:

> God brought the entire Conference down before Him in prayer that He would move upon the hearts of the authorities in Mexico to give permission for beginning work among this long neglected people. There are about two million Indians in that country who can be reached only in their own language.
>
> After further conference and prayer, it seemed wise that we ask Mr. W. C. Townsend, of Guatemala, to go to Mexico with us for the purpose of meeting with the authorities to get permission for sending men to these tribes to learn the languages and to translate the Bible into these tongues. (105)

The next day, one woman gave Legters a Whippet Six car so that he could drive to Mexico. Others gave money designated for gas and oil.

Legters was signed up for conferences in other states for the next two months, so it was October 26 before he and his wife left their home in Chambersburg. After holding conferences in Chattanooga and Birmingham, they drove to Dallas, where they had arranged to meet Cameron Townsend, who by now had fully recovered from tuberculosis.

On November 10, the three reached the Mexican border at Laredo, but suspicious immigration officials surmised that they were not ordinary pleasure-bound tourists. All churches in thirteen of Mexico's twenty-eight states were closed, and even Christian funerals were forbidden. Surely preachers could not be admitted to the country!

Undaunted, Legters prayed and hummed his favorite chorus, "Faith, Mighty Faith!" After several hours, the officials finally gave them permission to enter Mexico. However, the missionaries were warned that they would be fined 700 pesos and expelled immediately if Legters were caught preaching, or if Townsend were caught studying Indian languages.

In spite of the seemingly impossible restrictions, the travelers claimed the promises which they found in their *Daily Light* reading for the next morning, "Behold, I send an angel before thee, to keep thee in the way and to bring thee into the place which I have prepared."

Encouraged by God's Word, Mr. and Mrs. Legters and Townsend proceeded to Tamazunchale, where they were joined by Dr. and Mrs. Dale and their son John. The six then drove on to Mexico City to make their petition to the authorites. Edna Legters later reported:

> After two days of prayer and conference concerning the main object of our trip, we presented the Government on November 18 a petition requesting the privilege of bringing specially trained young men into the country to learn the languages of the 43 tribes of Indians, and to make grammars and dictionaries for the purpose of translating the New Testament into these tongues. What precious times followed as day after day the six of us waited before the Lord expecting the walls of our Jericho to fall down, and how graciously He spoke to us out of His Word! (106)

A month later, a disappointed Legters learned that permission had been refused. The government would not allow translators into the country. But at the same time, through some unusual and providential contacts with men in high places, Cameron Townsend was authorized to enter Mexico as an individual, for the purpose of studying its tribes.

While Legters traveled north for a conference ministry in Texas, Virginia, and Pennsylvania in early 1934, Townsend, armed with his miraculous government permit, began a six-weeks' tour of rural schools in Chiapas, Campeche and Yucatán. He interviewed students and teachers, and began compiling word lists from several Indian languages.

When word came that Elvira, whom he had left in Chicago, was seriously ill, he returned to the United States. Seeking a better climate for her, he moved to Sulphur Springs, Arkansas, and began making plans for the summer training camp which he and Legters were establishing.

The camp—which was planned to run from June 7 to September 7—had a very small beginning. In South Carolina, Townsend picked up Ed Sywulka, Legters' eager young recruit. Packed into Townsend's little Star, Ed and Joe Chicol (Townsend's young Cakchiquel helper) accompanied Cam to Sulphur Springs, where the camp was to be held on a nine-acre abandoned farm about a mile out of town.

Then Richmond McKinney, the second student, arrived from Dallas Seminary. Although Ed Sywulka wrote his brother that "about eight fellows are expected," the camp never reached those proportions. Yet even with only two full-time students, Legters and Townsend refused to be discouraged.

Everything was informal. There was no need for tuition money or even for an application. The campers chopped wood, pumped water, made beds out of boards and mattresses from grasses, and attended classes. Legters lectured on the Victorious Christian Life, Chicol introduced the students to Spanish, and Townsend taught Cakchiquel grammar and methods of reaching Indians. Sywulka reported that while he didn't have to study for Legters' classes, he found the structure of Cakchiquel with its 30,000 verb forms to be plenty challenging academically.

The camp did not even have a name when it began. A few days after classes had started, Sywulka wrote to friends:

Greetings from Camp Wycliffe, We have chosen this name in honor of the great English Bible translator because each of us hopes to follow his example among the Indians of Latin America. (107)

By the end of the summer there were four students, if one counted Joe Chicol, who was also a part-time teacher. The four concluded their summer's training in California, taking phonetics classes from Dr. Elbert McCreery, a former translator and missionary to Africa who had joined the faculty of the Bible Institute of Los Angeles. The first "Camp Wycliffe" had given the young men far more than instruction in grammar, anthropology and phonetics. Legters inspired them to believe God for the impossible as his booming voice led out in the the camp theme song:

"Faith, mighty faith, the promise sees, and looks to God alone.
Laughs at impossibilities, and cries, It shall be done!"

Townsend set an example of earnest intercession in group prayer meetings, and the lack of financial underwriting gave the students practical experience in trusting God for their daily bread.

That fall Sywulka and Chicol headed for Guatemala, as has already been noted. Legters continued with his conference and fund-raising ministry. Townsend looked after his sick wife, wrote a novel about the needs of the Latin American Indians, and waited and prayed for God to open more doors.

The next summer the student body at Camp Wycliffe grew to five. Richmond McKinney was back for another session. The new students were red-haired Bill Sedat, blond Maxwell Lathrop, and lanky Ken Pike, who hitchhiked all the way from Connecticut to Arkansas. There was one more trainee—David

Brainerd Legters, Leonard's only son. Just before graduating from Westminister Seminary he had written to Paul Burgess:

> The Indian work has been on my heart ever since I was a youngster and I know the Lord has a place for me there. Next May I graduate and plan on spending the summer in the "Training Camp for Bible Translators" in Arkansas which was initiated by my father last summer. Possibly you know something of the camp already, so I will not go into details about it, other than to say that it aims to prepare men physically as well as mentally to dig a primitive language out of a primitive people." (108

L. L. Legters recruited scores of young people for pioneer work, and each one brought him a sense of satisfaction. But surely he must have felt a very special joy to see his own son among the enthusiastic volunteers which would be supported by the Pioneer Mission Agency.

The senior Legters himself came again for two weeks of lecturing on anthropology and the Victorious Christian Life. Dr. E. L. McCreery taught phonetics. Young Joe Chicol was back to teach Indian customs and Cakchiquel, while Townsend taught the remaining classes.

But the door to Mexico had still not opened. Late in June the campers and staff met for a day of prayer that God would work a miracle in the Mexican government. As they knelt around the empty nail kegs which they used as chairs, they asked God once again to open the door for Bible translators to enter that country.

God answered in a wonderful way. That very afternoon a radio broadcast gave them the startling news: Mexico's president had dismissed the anti-Christian members of his cabinet! Now Townsend was sure that he could get permission to take linguists into the country.

When camp closed, Sedat proceeded to Guatemala and the other four students entered Mexico with Cameron and Elvira Townsend. After three weeks, Max Lathrop and Brainerd Legters returned briefly to the United States to be married, but Ken Pike stayed on in Mexico to work among the Mixtec Indians.

Later, he married Cameron's niece Evelyn, who had come with the Townsends to care for Elvira, by then practically an invalid. Four of the five members of the class of 1935 became lifelong translators or linguists. Richmond McKinney went to Mexico under the Southern Presbyterians, but only gave five years to tribal work. Bill Sedat, initially sponsored by the Pioneer Mission Agency and later by the Nazarenes, went on to translate the New Testament for the Kekchí people of Guatemala. Maxwell Lathrop was destined to become a Wycliffe translator for Mexico's Tarascan people, and Ken Pike would not only become a Bible translator himself, but also a scholar who would aid hundreds of other young translators through the years.

Brainerd Legters spent over a half century among the large Maya tribe in Yucatán, translating the New Testament, establishing churches, and raising up a camp and Bible teaching ministry. His son David joined him in the work and is following in his footsteps.

Some mention should be made of Gene Nida, who studied at S.I.L. in 1936, the third session. Along with Ken Pike, he is one of the best known S.I.L. students from the early days. The two of them directed S.I.L. together for many years. Later, Nida joined the United Bible Societies, where his ministry in the field of Bible translation literally circled the globe.

The third Camp Wycliffe had almost three times as many students as the second. From then on, the effort snowballed. At first, the young translators were supported primarily through the Pioneer Mission Agency. But the Agency was not a mission board as such; it was only a recruiting and fund-channeling organization. Legters reminded Townsend that the P.M.A. could not continue to send support to the translators unless they organized themselves formally.

Prompted by Legters, Townsend and several of his students worked with a Mexican lawyer and formed a new organization—The Summer Institute of Linguistics—in 1936. The

Council of the Pioneer Mission Agency acted as advisors for the new mission, until the work grew to such an extent that the P.M.A. asked Townsend to establish his own Board of Directors.

As the work grew, the Summer Institute of Linguistics gradually became independent of its parent organization, the Pioneer Mission Agency. But Legters continued to hold the work of Townsend and his fellow-translators close to his heart. And as Field Secretary for the P.M.A., he kept on raising funds and channeling them to the growing corps of young translators. (It was not until after Legters' death that it became logistically impossible for the Pioneer Mission Agency to continue to forward funds to the S.I.L. workers, and it was not until 1942 that Wycliffe Bible Translators was formally incorporated in California.)

In his conference ministry, Legters continued to hammer away at the need of pioneering, of translating the Bible, and of evangelizing the unreached peoples of the world. No one knows exactly how many young people he recruited for pioneer work, but Townsend estimated that because of Legters, "several hundred young people have gone into Christian work and a very large percentage of them to peoples who had never before heard the Message of Salvation." (109)

Legters must have felt a great deal of joy to see new translators enter the very tribes which he had surveyed and for which he had been praying for nearly twenty years. He continued to travel and speak in Victorious Life Conferences, but for some reason he felt led to accept no speaking engagements after May 1940.

That month he was scheduled to speak in a Baptist Church in Porterville, California. On Sunday, May 12, he preached on the Victorious Christian life with his usual vitality and then suggested "Lord, I'm Coming Home" as the invitation hymn. A few hours later, he suffered a massive heart attack, and within six days he was in the presence of the Lord.

Legters' work was over, but the vision which he and eleven others had dreamed and prayed for in Chichicastenango was being fulfilled.

In 1921 Dinwiddie wrote:

> It has not been my expectation that the foundation of this Latin American Indian Mission would be born overnight. What the Lord has done so far has been to suggest to me that He is laying the basis for a deep-seated, permanent and extensive work in which the spiritual people, both in the denominations and in the independent missions, will be linked together in a common task. (110)

If Dinwiddie and Legters were alive today, they would surely agree that their dream of a "deep-seated, permanent and extensive" work of reaching ethnic minorities around the world with God's Word in their own tongue has come wonderfully true. The legacy of the "Chichicastenango Twelve" lives on.

APPENDIX A. Part I:

The Minutes of the Meeting Proper

4\ January 23rd, 1921

5\ In response to a call sent out to the following missionaries urging them to meet Mr. H. B. Dinwiddie and Mr. Legters at Chichicastenango, all assembled in the home of A. B. Treichler: Mr. and Mrs. Paul Burgess, Mr. and Mrs. Herbert W. Toms, Mr. and Mrs. W. Cameron Townsend, Mr. William E. Robinson, Mr. and Mrs. Treichler and Miss Williams.

6\ Mr. Robinson offered a prayer for definite blessing and guidance from God in the conference to which we had been called to consider the best way to evangelize the Indians.

7\ Mr. Townsend then stated that apropos of the utterly neglected condition of 3,000,000 Indians in Mexico; 30,000,000 Indians in South America besides the great number of Guatemalan Indians and those of the other Central American republics, that God had reminded him of Psalm 119:126—"It is time for Jehovah to work", in the evangelization of the Indians of all Latin America in this generation, and that this conference should consider first—The Local Problem, and second—The Latin American Problem.

8\ On motion of Mr. Robinson, Mr. Burgess was appointed Chairman of the Conference. Unanimously carried.

9\ On motion of Mr. Townsend Mrs. Treichler was appointed Secretary of the Conference.

10\ Thereupon it was decided, on motion of Mr. Dinwiddie, that it is the sense of the meeting that the Indian problems be discussed freely and that the members of the Conference make suggestions to clarify our understanding of the Indian need and that we undertake to discuss these phases of the work in their order of importance. Unanimously carried.

11\ Mr. Townsend presented for discussion the question—"Can the Indians of Guatemala be evangelized in this generation according to the present methods?"

12\ Mr. Dinwiddie offered a prayer for a definite recognition of the Lord's will by all the members of the Conference.

13\ The Chairman spoke of the work already established among Indians here in Guatemala and the stamp of the Lord's blessing upon it and asked for suggestions as to methods of procedure.

14\ Mr. Dinwiddie presented for comparison the following figures: With about 10,000 Ladino believers the average arrives at about twenty to one, as compared with the Indian population. He also stated as elements of this situation: the retiring nature of the Indians; that Indians usually enter Ladino congregations mainly with an idea of becoming Ladino themselves; the military service as a factor in the disintegration of the Indian civilization. As an argument for the plan to evangelize the Indians in their own tongues, Mr. Dinwiddie stated that the trade language of Africa, (where there are hundreds of tribal languages) is of no use in evangelizing.

15\ Then followed discussion as to the inadequacy of Indian languages to express all religious thought. Mr. Burgess argued in favor of putting the Scriptures in the Indian languages.

16\ Mr. Dinwiddie asked if any people had ever been evangelized except in their own tongue, which the meeting were forced to answer negatively.

17\ Mr. Legters then stated that in order to know God's will we have only to look at what God is doing already.

18\ Mr. Dinwiddie mentioned the rule of the British Government which compels all of its officials in India to study the literature and home life and lore of the natives. A British Army officer visiting Mexico was impressed and shocked by the imposition inflicted by the Spanish people upon the Indians and stated that the Mexicans will never manage their Indian population by their present methods.

19\ Mr. Burgess suggested the importance of guarding against political trouble in doing Indian work.

20\ Mr. Townsend suggested translations with parallel readings in Spanish and Indian.

21\ Mr. Legters called attention to the fact that the only way to reach this generation of Indians is in their own tongues.

22\ Mr. Toms asked if a translation of the Bible for the San Antonio Indians would serve for other Cachequels.

23\ Mr. Townsend replied that it would only serve for 150,000 Cachequels.

24\ Mr. Toms raised the question as to whether the best way to reach Indians is to translate the Bible into the Indian languages or to reach them thru [sic] Spanish speaking Indians.

Trailblazers for Translators

25\ Mr. Legters suggested that the Indians have not the training to read a Spanish Bible and understand it clearly because of their limited knowledge of Spanish.

26\ Mr. Legters asked for prayer as to the Lord's will about the Indians of this generation having the Gospel in their own tongue. Mr. Legters led in this prayer.

27\ Mr. Toms raised the question of the present translation into Quiché of the Gospel of Mark and the Gospel of Luke into the Cachequel, as to whether they have proved useful or not in evangelizing Indians.

28\ Mr. Legters moved that it is the sense of this body that although present methods have reached a certain number of Indians, that the Indians of Guatemala should have the Gospel of the Lord Jesus Christ in a written form in their own languages.

29\ On motion of Mr. Dinwiddie, the meeting adjourned for the night with prayer.

30\ January 24th, 1921
31\ The Chairman opened the meeting by asking for requests for prayer and, after receiving definite requests as to the personal needs of the members present, the meeting went to prayer.

32\ The Chairman then announced that our first topic for consideration for the day is to discuss and decide upon methods for reaching Indians in their own languages.

33\ Mr. Townsend asked Mr. Burgess if he could study the Indian language while living in Quezaltenango. Mr. Burgess replied that he finds it impossible to acquire the Indian tongue without living among Indians and that men must be separated for this particular work.

34\ Mr. Legters asked how this is to be accomplished. Mr. Burgess stated that missionaries must be prayed out who will live and learn right with the Indians. Mr. Legters called attention to the fact that Peter and Paul got together to decide how the work was to be done and they decided that the whole business of Paul was with evangelizing the Gentiles and of Peter the Jews, and that we must well recognize the importance of rightly dividing the work between the workers.

35\ Mr. Dinwiddie asked why Mr. Burgess and Mr. Townsend did not arrange during their anticipated stay of a couple of months among the Indians in their respective fields to translate the same Gospel and compare notes afterward.

36\ Mr. Townsend suggested beginning with "Porciones Escogidas"; Mr. Robinson wants to begin with the Quiché translation of Mark, selecting all Cachequel words which occur in that work.

37\ Mr. Burgess stated that it will be necessary to observe uniform rules by all who work on the translations.

38\ On motion of Mr. Legters, it was resolved that Mr. Burgess and Mr. Townsend constitute themselves a Translating Committee that they translate the Gospel separately and afterward come together to compare their translations. Unanimously carried.

39\ Mr. Robinson then invited Messrs. Burgess and Townsend to Panajachel next September for this comparison.

40\ The following remarks were then considered: That it is quite easy for Mr. Herbert Toms to lean an Indian language, having a perfect pronunciation of the Spanish. Mr. Frank Toms not able to manage their present large work alone.

41\ Indians must be trained to do the work, but at least two missionaries should work with each tribe. Mr. Robinson touches 85,000 Cachiquels in his department; there are 150,000 Cachiquels in Mr. Townsend's district; there are 60,000 Cachiquels in in Totonicopan; there are 60,000 Cachiquels in Quezaltenango.

42\ There should be a missionary family for Totonicopan. There are over 300,000 Cachiquels in Guatemala.

43\ In Quezaltenango there are also Mams, but there must be one special missionary given to them, so as not to mix up the different tribes.

44\ Mr. Burgess stated that he cannot look to his Board to support Indian workers.

45\ It was also stated that in Mexico there is one tribe which the Mexican Government makes no pretense of ever having conquered.

46\ In Nicaragua the Moravian Mission have 7000 members of their church.

47\ The Indians of Del Norte need one missionary couple; the Mam tribe one couple; the Quichés two couples; the Cachiquels one couple; the Quechis [Kekchi?] one couple; the Cobans two couples, and two single missionaries are needed for Townsend in the district of the Cachiquels. There are 200,000 Mams.

48\ In order to begin the foundation work of giving the Gospel to the Indians in their different languages for the Republic of Guatemala, there are needed at the present time seven couples and two single women and two additional couples to relieve missionaries now occupied in Ladino work for the Indian work. This was then made a motion, seconded and unanimously passed.

49\ On motion the meeting adjourned with prayer.

50\ January 24th, 1921 (Evening session)

51\ The conference reconvened after dinner, and after prayer the Chairman announced that the meeting had before it for consideration The Method of Organization, the auspices under which the new recruits for whom we are praying are to come to the field.

52\ Mr. Burgess asked if there should be a separate organization for Indian work in Guatemala, known as The Latin American Indian Mission. Mr. Dinwiddie said he considered it a pity to have a separate organization if things could be aranged without it.

53\ It was then discussed and decided that the Guatemalan Indian is our first problem; the next problem those of Mexico and lastly—the South American Indians, and that if God should give any of us a personal conviction of an interest beyond our present sphere of work, we would join in carrying it out.

54\ Mr. Burgess stated that we are not limited to our own immediate sphere but that our work is related to a much greater problem.

55\ Mr. Dinwiddie stated tht his conviction is that God is going to work for the Latin American Indian and that, in order to do effective work, each one of us must have a vision of working and praying for the larger field. He also stated that there is in So. America a little work in Ecuador, a little in Bolivia, and that in Paraguay there is a work which was intended for Indians but which became absorbed in Spanish work; also there is an existing work of the Church of England in Paraguay and Bolivia.

56\ Mr. Dinwiddie also stated that in going over the existing unevangelized fields and their possible source of supply from the denominations, he had found that there is only one pioneer work to be undertaken this year by them, and that is in Abyssinia.

57\ The Chairman then called upon the meeting for personal expressions as to the character of any organization for the evangelization of the Latin Indians.

58\ Mr. Townsend suggested an organization with a generous policy but giving the Indian first place

59\ Mr. Robinson said he would like to be in a prayer circle to pray for the Latin American Indians and to feel that there is one solid organization for the evangelization of all the Indians, with our native congregations contributing toward the larger work.

60\ Mr. Toms thought an organization devoted to evangelizing all the Indians of Latin America would be of great help to local stations and deepen their zeal and spirit.

61\ Mr. Legters stated that when God starts things he has great things in view.

62\ Thereupon, on motion of Mr. Dinwiddie, it was resolved that it is the sense of this conference that in view of the fact that the problem of the unevangelized Indians is one and the same throughout Latin America, it would be desirable that a body be formed which, by contribution, by cooperation, by direct activity would evangelize the Indians of Latin America, reported to be over 40,000,000 in number. Unanimously carried.

63\ This body would contribute to the direct organization, it would cooperate with others and engage in direct activity where the work was undone.

64\ The members of this body who had knowledge of Indian work could be of immense value to new missionaries who wanted to go to pioneer fields.

65\ Mr. Dinwiddie stated that no individual missionary can give all the necessary information; it is collective experience that will get the work done.

66\ Mr. Townsend said it had been found that allmost [sic] the only missionaries who have gone forth from Guatemala have been Indians. Chiquimula Mission have sent six Indian missionaries to Honduras. These Indian missionaries opened up the trail between Chiquimula and Tegucigalpa.

67\ The matter of necessary Committees was discussed and it was suggested that the following committees be appointed:

68\ A Committee to look after occupation of territory and cooperation with other missions, (If volunteers offered, they might become members of the missions already occupying the field) and to incite to greater activity the missions responsible for work already existing.

69\ A committee of organization;
70\ A committee on Policy and Doctrine (The relation of the native brethren to this work shall be defined by the Committee on Policy).
71\ A committtee on Women's and Children's work.
72\ It was moved and unanimously carried that the appointment of committees be left to the Chair.
73\ Mr. Burgess then appointed the following Committees: Committee on Occupation and Cooperation: Mr. Burgess,. Mr. Townsend, Mr. Toms
74\ Committee on Organization: Mr. Dinwiddie, Mr. Legters, Mr. Robinson, Mrs. Treichler
75\ Committee on Doctrine and Policy: Mr. Treichler, Mr. Legters, Mr. Toms
76\ Committee on Women's and Children's Work: Miss Williams, Mrs. Toms, Mrs. Burgess, Mrs. Townsend
77\ Adjourned with prayer.

[Jan 25th AM—Committees at work]

78\ January 25th, 1921
79\ The conference reconvened at 3 p.m., and after prayer, the Chairman called for the Report of the Committee on Occupation and Cooperation.
80\ It was moved and unanimously resolved that no report should be acted upon until all reports should have been read.
81\ Mr. Toms then read the report of the Committee on Occupation and Cooperation, as follows:
82\ "In the matter of cooperation, the policy of this organization is to incite the various Mission Boards responsible for centers to undertake the adequate manning of the same. Wherever practicable, this organization will work thru [sic] the established agencies, seeking to aid them to procure recruits and funds for them. Where an established agency does not undertake the adequate reaching of the Indians, nor cares to do so, this organization will feel at liberty to occupy the field, if possible with the consent of the organizations already occupying the territory.
83\ "Since the object of this organization is to evangelize in the shortest possible time the Latin American Indians, it expresses its sincere willingness to

cooperate with all sound, evangelical societies at work on the fields and expresses its willingness to turn over such work as it may have established when these organizations mentioned are equipped adequately to carry on the work along the lines laid down.
84\ "As a matter of general principle, the unit of endeavor shall be tribal and this condition or consideration will determine the division of territory."
85\ "Suggestions for the placing of Indian workers:
86\ For the Mam tribe
    1   San Pedro Sacatepequez
87\ 2   San Ildefonzo Ixtahuacan
88\ For Del Norte Tribe
    3   San Miguel Acatan
89\ For Cachiquel Tribe
    4   Quezaltenango for Quezaltenango, Such. and Retalileu
90\ 5   Totonicopan for Totonicopan and north of Quezaltenango
    6   Panajachel for Sololá and part of Such.
91\ For Quiché Tribe
    8   Santo Tomás
92\ 9   Zacualpa
For [Kekchi]
    10 Near Cobán
93\ 11 Near Salamá
94\ Mr. Dinwiddie then read the draft of the report of the Committee on Organization, and stated that the prevailing idea is field direction.
95\   I.
96\   Name
97\ "The name of this association shall be _____.

98\   II.
99\   Object
100\ The object of this association shall be, by contribution to and cooperation with other agencies and also by direct activity, to give the Gospel to the Indians of Latin America.

101\   III.
102\   General Direction
103\ The management and direction of this association shall be vested in a General Council; the local government in a Field and Home Councils under the General Council.

104\   IV.
105\ Members of General Council

106\ The General Council shall be composed of all members of the Association both in Home and Field Councils.

107\ V.
108\ Members of Field Councils
109\ The members of the Field Councils shall consist only of those 1—Who believe they have been called of God to devote themselves primarily to the evangelization of the Indians of Latin America; 2—Those who subscribe annually in writing to the doctrinal belief of the Association as their personal conviction; 3—Those who have had experience in the winning of souls and are actively engaged to that end; whose lives are surrendered to Christ as Lord and who reveal by the working of the Holy Spirit in them as examples to others the character of Christ in their service and everyday living; who work in hearty accord with the policies and practices of the Association as expressed by its general and local Councils.

110\ VI.
111\ Members of Home Council
112\ The members of the Home Council shall be those only who believe that God has called them to give a contribution in prayer and service to the evangelization of the Indians of Latin America as one of the important parts of their service under Him; those who subscribe annually in writing to the doctrinal belief of the Association as their personal conviction; those who have had experience in the winning of souls and are actively engaged to that end; whose lives are surrendered to Christ as Lord and who reveal by the working of the Holy Spirit in them as examples to others the character of Christ in their service and everday living; and who work in hearty accord with the policies and practices of the Association as expressed by its General and Local Councils.

113\ VII.
114\ Officers
115\ There shall be the following officers of the General Council—Chairman, Secretary, Treasurer and General Director. These officers shall compose the Executive Committee of the General Council, which shall have power to act for the Council between its meetings in accordance with the principles and policies adopted by the Council.

116\ The Chairman shall preside at the meetings of the General Council.
117\ The Secretary shall be responsible for the Minutes, keeping of records and correspondence relating to the meetings of the Council.
118\ The General Director shall be the general executive agent of the General Council.
119\ The Treasurer shall be responsible for the receipt and disbursement of all monies of the Mission in accordance with the policy of the Mission, instruction of the General Council and of its Executive Committee.
120\ Officers of the Field Council shall consist of Chairman, Secretary, Field Treasurer.
121\ The Chairman shall preside at meetings of the Field Council and shall have general supervision and responsibility for the interests of the Mission in his field.
122\ The Treasurer shall receive and disburse the funds of the Association for his field in accordance with the principles and instructions of the General Council and of the decisions of the Field Councils in conformity therewith.
123\ The Secretary shall be responsible for the Minutes of meetings and correspondence relating to the general correspondence of the Field Council.
124\ A field council shall be organized in any field which in the judgment of the General Council or its Executive Committee is ready for such organization. Until a field council shall be organized the conduct of the work on each field shall be under the direction of the General Council thru [sic] its General Director.
125\ Members of the Field Council shall be elected by the Field Council in accordance with the conditions of membership of the Association. Such members shall have the right to take part in the meetings and discussions of the Field Council but shall not have power to vote until they have been on the field at least for two years anbd shall have been accepted by the Field Council as voting members.
126\ The Officers of the Home Council shall be Chairman, Treasurer, Recording Secretary and Executive Secretary.
127\ The function of the Chairman shall be to preside at the meetings of the Home Council and to see that the Home Council is conducted in accordance with the general policies of the Association.
128\ The function of the Treasurer shall be to receive funds and disburse them in

143

accordance with the rule of the General Council.

129\ The Executive Secretary shall be the executive officer of the Home Council in the country for which the Council is created and shall present the needs of the Latin American Indians, inform the Executive Committee of the General Council of the transactions of the Home Council and other matters of importance. He shall receive the applications of candidates for the Mission Field and examine these candidates and bring before the Home Council information relative to their calling and qualifications for the field."

130\ On motion of Mr. Legters, the draft of the report of the Committee on Organization was reread and considered section by section:

131\ Name It was unanimously resolved that the name of the Association should be The Latin American Indian Mission.

132\ Object It was unanimously resolved to approve the object of this Association as stated in the Organization Committee's report.

133\ Membership Mr. Burgess asked if it would be well to insert a clause relative to a language test. Discussion ruled this out. Mr. Robinson asked if provision should be made to exclude [sic] new voting members from holding office, which point was not incorporated.

134\ January 25, 1921 (evening session)
135\ After a short season of prayer, Mr. Dinwiddie suggested that the officers of the General Council be identical with the officers of the Field Council for the time being, as Guatemala is the whole field at present.

136\ On motion of Mr. Legters, it was resolved to pass upon the various Articles of the Rules of Organization one by one as read.

137\ Name The Latin American Indian Mission. Unanimously carried.

138\ Object Unanimously approved as read.

139\ General Council Approved unanimously as read.

140\ Members of General Council
Mr. Dinwiddie stated that the number of the members of the Home Council will be limited to nine. Approved unanimously as read.

141\ Each Field Council shall be composed of all members of the Mission in its given field; its function shall be to plan and prosecute the work in its given territory. Unanimously approved.

142\ Members of Field Council approved as read.

143\ Members of Home Council approved as read.

144\ Officers approved as read.

145\ Field Councils approved as read

146\ Section 1 Members of Field Council
147\ approved as read.

148\ Section 2 Members of Home Council
149\ approved as read.

150\ On motion of Mr. Townsend, the report of the Organization Committee was adopted as a basis of organization and beginning of activity and Mr. Dinwiddie was appointed a Committee of one to go over it with the reports of the other Committees and the opinions which we have expressed and submit to us later in fuller detail—(especially as to By-laws, which have not been formed as yet) matters relating to operation. Unanimously carried.

151\ It was also decided that the report of the Organization Committee be sent to each individual member of the Association and a vote submitted to the local chairman. Unanimously carried.

152\ Mr. Legters reported that the report on Policy had not been completed.

153\ The report on Doctrinal Basis was then read, as follows:

154\ "WE BELIEVE

155\ In ONE GOD, revealed as existing in three equal persons, Father, Son and Holy Spirit.

156\ In the full inspiration of the Old and New Testament.

157\ In the virgin birth of the Lord Jesus Christ, His substitutionary suffering on the cross as the only means of salvation from sin and His bodily resurrection for our justification.

158\ In the assurance of salvation thru [sic] the finished work of Christ.

159\ In salvation by faith without works, but good works as a manifestation of our faith.

160\ We are united in the hope of the imminent bodily return of our Lord.

161\ In the indwelling of the Spirit in every believer and filling for life and service to those who are yielded to Him.

162\ In the will, power and the providence of God to meet our every need.

163\ In the future state of unending blessedness for the saved with Christ and the state of unending conscious suffering for the lost.

164\ In His present position as the Head of the Church and the Lord and the Life of every believer.

165\ That the primary responsibility of every believer is that of bringing men to accept Christ as their personal Saviour."

166\ On motion of Mr. Robinson the Doctrinal Policy was adopted after such modifications of a literary character should be made of the original draft as are necessary. Unanimously carried.

167\ The report of the Committee on Occupation was then reread and on motion of Mr. Robinson was approved unanimously.

168\ The report of the Committee on Work for Women and Children was then read, as follows:

169\ "It is absolutely necessary for the missionary women engaged in Indian work to learn the Indian dialect. Bible classes or any special work for the women cannot be commenced until the missionary can speak their language. It is very seldom that an Indian woman understands the Spanish language.

170\ Where possible the wife should accompany her husband on evangelization trips. It serves in bringing the women together and also they lose the false idea that it is a religion for men only.

171\ Indian Bible women are needed. They can in their own tongue do a great work in house to house visitation, and can be used of God in bringing the women to the Lord in a way that would be impossible for a foreigner.

172\ The missionary's heart should be filled with a very special love, and be ready to help these poor ignorant women in things concerning themselves and their homes. Especially should they be willing to teach them how to care for their children. Mrs. Toms spoke of a series of letters on how to care for babies, written by a missionary in China. These should be translated into the Indian dialect and given to mothers.

173\ THE CHILDREN: Schools should be established in the most important towns. They should be conducted by native teachers. The children should have the first hour each morning in Bible study, to be conducted in the Indian tongue, copies of the Scriptures being in the hands of each child. Thus they are taught to read the Scriptures in their own tongue, so that in their homes they may be able to give the Word of God to the entire family, acquainting them with the Scriptures in their native tongue. This will also prevent the children from forgetting the dialect even when learning the Spanish language. The children should not be permitted to use the dialect during school hours outside of this Bible study class.

174\ An American teacher should be located in a Mission center. She should occupy herself in training more advanced pupils as teachers. She should superintend schools in her district and should very [sic] three months visit one of the schools in her district, having all teachers from other towns meet with her in that particular place for conference with the teachers as well as to inform herself as to actual conditions in the school. Of course for each conference with the teachers should would [sic] meet with them in the different schools in the district. This would mean an advance in the schools in the district, as well as be a great blessing to the teachers having this personal touch with the missionary.

175\ Wherever Sunday Schools are opened, classes for the children should be organized."

176\ Whereupon, the foregoing report was on motion of Mr. Robinson, adopted as read.

177\ The Chairman then announced that the status of the Mission as to its working on a faith basis or not, should be discussed, and also whether the workers will be guaranteed their support or whether the Council will uphold the worker in prayer for his support.

178\ On motion of Mr. Legters, it was resolved that a Committee of two be appointed (of which Mr. Dinwiddie should be one) to prepare a policy for a financial basis of the Mission, which shall be incorporated with the report on Organization, and be submitted to the Mission when Mr. Dinwiddie has prepared it. Mr. Dinwiddie then asked Mrs. Burgess to serve with him on this Committee, and they retired from the meeting to prepare this policy.

179\ On motion of Mr. Townsend, it was decided to proceed with the organization of the Field Council, which shall function as a General Council to begin activities at home.

180\ The meeting then proceeded to the election of officers.

181\ On motion of Mr. Townsend, it was resolved to vote by ballot and the persons

Trailblazers for Translators

receiving the two highest number of ballots to receive the nomination.

182\ Thereupon a ballot was cast for Chairman resulting in a tie between Mr. Burgess and Mr. Townsend; a second ballot was taken showing a majority in favor of Mr. Burgess, which on motion was made unanimous.

183\ A ballot was then taken for secretary, resulting in a majority for Mrs. Treichler, which was also on motion made a unanimous vote.

184\ The balloting for Treasurer was then done, Mr. Robinson receiving the majority of votes, which on motion was made unanimous.

185\ The meeting then proceeded to elect officers for the General Council.

186\ Mr. Robinson then nominated Mr. Dinwiddie as General Director of the Latin American Indian Mission, and he was unanimously elected.

187\ Mr. Dinwiddie then reentered the meeting and the Chairman announced to Mr. Dinwiddie our earnest desire that he accept under God our call as General Director. Mr. Dinwiddie then expressed his entire willingness to do anything in his power for this Mission but requested time to pray with Mrs. Dinwiddie about the matter and to let us know later.

188\ On motion of Mr. Townsend, the meeting then resolved to ask Mr. Dinwiddie to act as Executive Secretary for the Home Council pending his acceptance of the General Directorship. Unanimously carried.

189\ On Motion [sic] of Mr. Townsend, it was resolved that the Chairman constitute a Committee of one to report on a publication to be issued in the States by this Mission, which was unanimously carried with the amendment to including Mr. Dinwiddie on the Committee, and suggesting the name "The Latin American Indian".

190\ On motion of Mr. Townsend, Mr. Legters was asked to serve on the Home Council. Unanimously carried.

191\ The meeting adjourned at twelve o'clock midnight after prayer. HALLELUJAH! "IT IS TIME FOR JEHOVAH TO WORK".

192\ H. Treichler,
193\ Secretary.

Appendix A. Part II.

194\ The following is a resumé of the devotional meetings of the Conference on the Evangelization of the Latin American Indians at Chichicastenango, January 23rd to 25th inclusive, 1921:

195\ At 9 o'clock each morning there was a special service for the missionaries and the Indian workers in the Chapel.

196\ At 2 o'clock each afternoon a Chapel service was held for the missionaries and the Indian workers in the Chapel.

197\ Each evening there was a special evangelistic service.

198\ On Sunday morning at 9 o'clock Mr. Dinwiddie spoke on "The Vision of Joshua of the Angel who came as the Prince leader of the People".

199\ On Sunday afternoon Mr. Legters spoke on "The Privilege of Sons", especially the privilege of the prayer life of the Sons.

200\ On Monday morning Mr. Legters spoke on "The Vision of Isaiah—How God Makes a Missionary—That God seeks Clean Sons". After this meeting the Indians remained in the Chapel to pray and the missionaries adjourned to the house parlor to pray for each other. We confessed our needs one to another and prayed for one another.

201\ On Monday afternoon Mr. Dinwiddie spoke on the subject of "Humble Sons for God's Service".

202\ On Tuesday morning, Mr. Legters spoke on the subject of Trusting Sons for God's Service and that today He is seeking to find sons who will trust him to the uttermost. After this meeting the Indians remained in the Chapel to pray and the missionaries adjourned to the house to pray and stated their personal needs. This merged into a consecration meeting and a presenting of ourselves to God to work in us and to make us trusting sons.

203\ On Tuesday afternoon Mr. Dinwiddie spoke on "The Priviliege of sons to bear each others' burdens before the throne of God".

204\ On Tuesday evening, after completing the business recounted on the Minutes, the missionaries again went to prayer until midnight.

205\ On Wednesday morning early, all the visitors except Mr. Legters, and Mrs. and Mrs. Townsend left for their respective homes.

Appendix A. Part III.

206\ The following is a list of requests for prayer received at the Conference on the evangelization of the Latin American Indians held at Chichicastenango, January 23rd to 25th inclusive, 1921:

207\ For the Department of Quiché—that a work may be raised up.

208\ Cipriano Alvarado requested prayer for himself and for the Indians in Sololá Department. (A worker with Treichlers).

209\ For the Indians of San Cristobal.

210\ That the number of believers in the Department of Quezaltenango be increased.

211\ Pray for the indifferent Indian believers in Cantel.

212\ Pray for believers in the district of Patzum that they may marry and arrange their lives.

213\ Pray about the hymnbook being gotten up in lengua at Quezaltenango; also that there may be closer communion amongst the brethren there.

214\ For San Lucas Tolimán that many may be saved.

215\ That souls may be saved among the Mams and Cachiquels.

216\ For San Antonio, that the workers may arrange things so as to be able to get out giving full time to the Lord, (1) for Flavio that his father may let him have full time; (2) for Bernardino that he may get married; (3) for Luis and his wife, as well as his mother and brother that they may not stand in his way, but that he may go out knowing that the Lord has definitely called him for service.

217\ For Daniel. Travels alone so much working in the fincas in the coast country. The district is immense and there are no other workers.

218\ San Marcos and Huehuetenango; workers for Indians and that the seed sown may bear fruit.

219\ Department of Sololá and Mr. Robinson that he may learn the lengua and that souls may be saved.

220\ For Nasario—many debts on hand, not living well, asks for increase of faith.

221\ Coatepeque, Mr. Burgess, chapel being built. Also for the hymnbook, pray for translators that the hymns may be translated correctly and that no false or erroneous ideas may enter in the hymns. (Lengua hymnbook)

222\ Tula asks for San Antonio and the lake towns.

223\ Quichés   Treichlers—pray for conversions among Indians.

224\ Quichés   Pray for an expert in language work for Quiché.

225\ Pray for a medical missionary amongst the Quichés.

226\ For missionaries from the USA.

227\ For Mr. Legters that His will be done.

228\ Brigido asks for school in San Antonio that the children may definitely come out for Christ, and for him as teacher that he may be such an example as the Lord wants.

229\ Pray for Santa Maria Palmar.

230\ Pray for women believers among the Indians that they may truly learn to know Him.

Appendix A. Part IV.

231\ ARTICLES
232\ for
233\ CONSTITUTION AND BYLAWS
234\ OF THE LATIN AMERICAN MISSION, (ADOPTED AS A BASIS FOR ACTIVITY UNTIL FINAL DRAFT SHALL HAVE BEEN PREPARED AND ADOPTED).

235\   I.
236\   NAME
237\ The name of this Association shall be THE LATIN AMERICAN INDIAN MISSION.

238\   II.

239\   OBJECT
240\ The object of this Mission shall be by contribution to and cooperation with other agencies, and also by direct activity, to give the Gospel to the Indians of Latin America.

241\   III.
242\ GENERAL DIRECTION
243\ There shall be a General Council of the Mission which shall determine its policies including the basis for the selction [sic] of its missionaries, receive the report of all its operations, thru [sic] its officers— have general supervision of the whole

work, elect its administrative officers and receive and administer all funds.

244\   IV.
245\   GENERAL COUNCIL
246\ The General Council shall be composed of all members of the Mission, both in the Home and the Field Councils.
247\ There shall be the following officers of the General Council—Chairman, Secretary, Treasurer and General Director.
248\ The Chairman shall preside over the meetings of the General Council.
249\ The Secretary shall be responsible for the Minutes, keeping of the records and correspondence relating to the meetings of the Council.
250\ The Treasurer shall be responsible for the receipts and disbursements of all monies of the Mission, in accordance with the policies of the Mission, and the instructions of the General Council and its executive officers.
251\ The General Director shall be the general executive agent of the General Council.
252\ The Officers of the General Council shall be the Executive Committee. The Executive Committee shall be responsible for the conduct of the general business and oversight of the Mission in accordance with the policies of the General Council and the principles of the Mission.

253\   V.
254\   THE FIELD COUNCIL
255\ Each Field Council shall be composed of all the Members of the Mission in its particular field. The function of a field councill [sic] shall be to plan and prosecute the work of the Mission within its territory, in conformity with the policies of the General Council and the principles of the Mission.
256\ Officers of a Field Council shall consist of Chairman, Secretary and Field Treasurer.
257\ A Field Council may be organized in any field which in the judgment of the General Council or its Executive Committee is ready for such organization. Until a Field Council shall be organized, the conduct of the work on each field shall be under the direction of the General Council thru [sic] its General Director.
258\ The Chairman shall preside at meetings of the Field Council and shall have general responsibility for the interests of the Mission in his field.

259\ The Treasurer shall receive and disburse the funds of the Mission for his field in accordance with the principles and instructions of the General Council and of the decisions of the Field Council in conformity therewith.
260\ The Secretary shall be responsible for the Minutes of the meetings and correspondence relating to the general business of the Field Council.

261\   VI.
262\   HOME COUNCILS
263\ A Home Council shall be composed of all the Members of the Mission in any territory which in the judgment of the General Council or of its Executive Committee, supporters of the Mission in prayer and otherwise are to be found. It shall be organized by the Executive Committee thru [sic] the General Director. Its functions shall be to promote the interests and conduct the work of the Mission in its particular territory, including making public the needs of the Indians of Latin America, the receiving and transmission of funds to the General Council, the receiving of applications of candidates for missionary service and the examination and acceptance or otherwise of each candidate, and especially the promotion of prayer for the Mission.
264\ The Officers of the Home Council shall be Chairman, Treasurer and Executive Secretary.
265\ The function of the Chairman shall be to preside at the meetings of the Home Council and to see that the business of the Home Council is conducted in accordance with the general principles of the Mission and the policies of the General Council.
266\ The function of the Treasurer shall be to receive and disburse funds in accordance with the instructions of the General Council.
267\ The Executive Secretary shall be the Executive Officer of the Home Council in the territory for which the General Council is created and shall present the needs of the Latin American Indians, inform the Executive Committee of the General Council of the transactions of the Home Council and other matters of importance. He shall receive the application of candidates for the Mission Field and bring before the Home Council information relative to their calling and qualifications for the field.

268\ VII.
269\ MEMBERS OF THE MISSION
270\ Members of the Mission shall consist only of members of the Home and Field Councils whose condition of Membership shall differ in the first of the following particulars only.
271\ [sic] Members of the Field Council including its officers shall consist only of those who believe they have been called of God to devote themselves primarily to the evangelization of the Indians of Latin America. All members shall subscribe annually in writing to the doctrinal belief of the Mission as their personal conviction. All members shall have had experience in the winning of souls to Christ as Saviour and be actively engaged to that end. All members shall have surrendered to Christ as Lord and reveal by the working of the Holy Spirit in them as examples to others the character of Christ in their service and everyday living. All members shall work in hearty accord with the principles and policies and practices of the Mission as expressed by its General and their respective Field and Home Councils.
272\ Members of the Home Council including its officers shall be those only who believe that God has called them to give a contribution in prayer and service to the evangelization of the Indians of Latin America as one of the important parts of their service under Him.
273\ Members of the Field Councils shall be elected by the Field Council in accordance with the conditions of membership of the Mission. Such members shall have a right to take part in the meetings and discussions of the Field Council, but shall not have power to vote until they have been on the field at least for two years and shall have been accepted by the Field Council as voting members.
274\ Members of a Home Council shall be nominated by the Home Council and shall be approved by the General Council or its Executive Committee. The number of members for any particular Home Council shall not exceed nine.

275\ VIII.
276\ FINANCIAL BASIS
277\ The financial basis of the Mission shall be to depend utterly upon the infallible faithfulness of God to provide for the needs of His servants in the work to which He has called them. The responsibility of the Officers and Members of the Councils shall be to keep informed as to the sufficiency of funds in the Treasury and to be faithful in prayer, life, service and personal giving for the needs of the workers.
278\ There shall be no guarantee of funds beyond what is in the treasury and no debts incurred.
279\ (The Executive Secretaries and the General Director shall be on the same financial basis as the missionaries.)

149

Dialogue of the "Chichicastenango Twelve"
at the formation of the Latin American Indian Mission, Jan 23-25, 1921.

Note: The name, age, and *date of arrival* in Guatemala are listed below, others were present, but their comments were not recorded.

Key: △ = prayed, Ⓣ = talked, Ⓜ = motion, shaded areas are afternoon/evening sessions.

January 23, Evening

Discussion

Continued...

Legters, 48, Visitor—Experience in Indian work in USA from 1903, convinced of need to use Indian languages

Dinwiddie, 44, Visitor—A godly businessman turned Victorious Life renewal preacher, giving deeper life conference in Guatemala

Burgesses, 35, 1913—Planted 70 Spanish churches, deeply concerned for 75% Indian pop., learning Quiche as possible (Presbyterian)

Robinson, 35, 1920—College friend of Townsend, also doing Indian work (CAM-Central American Mission, today CAM Intl.)

Toms, 30, 1911—Missionary kid, absorbed in his father's work with the Spanish, but concerned also about the Indian majority (CAM).

Townsends, 25, 1917—Cam had just married a Presb. Missionary, was originally a Bible Colporter, then joined CAM mission.

The following comments refer to the numbered events above which, in turn, refer to the numbered paragraphs in Appendix A, Parts I-IV.

7. The youngest male present, Townsend, was the first to speak, introducing at the outset the plight of Native Americans in all of Latin America ("30 million") adding the characteristic Student Volunteer Movement's phrase "in this generation."

9. Townsend was also the first to make a motion, albeit trivial, as to who was to be the recording secretary.

11. Again he spoke up to phrase a formal purpose for the conference in the form of a question: "Can the Indians of Guatemala be evangelized in this generation according to the present methods?" Bur-

gess, Legters, and even Dinwiddie had a great deal of previous experience and thinking to bring to the discussion.

15. It is remarkable at this late date in history after centuries of Bible translation that Indian languages would be questioned as adequate "to express all religious thought."

33. Townsend is again the first to speak the second day. You see here the 40-48. You see here the

clear tension between Spanish and Indian work.

52. First reference to a name for the mission that emerged from the discussion. However, note that Dinwiddie hopes existing organizations will be able to do the job.

53. The unfulfilled pledge here is that if "any of us" were drawn into a sphere larger than Guatemala the rest "would join in carrying it

150

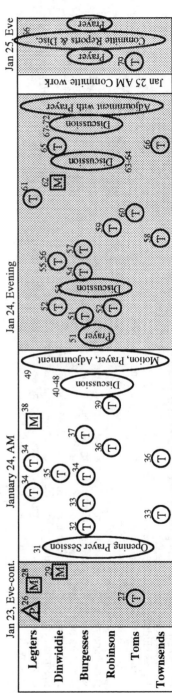

out." Years later when both Townsend and Legters launched what became Wycliffe Bible Translators, they apparently could not, and did not, depend on the others in this group.

56. It is possible that Dinwiddie here refers to the mainline denominational boards, which by 1921 had apparently already developed their field work beyond the pioneer stage—with a single exception!

60. The one second-generation missionary felt that a hemispheric organization would significantly encourage local work in any one country.

62. (Note: now speaking of *40 million* Indians!) With the backing of Legters and Dinwiddie, the group moved decisively to a hemispheric entity. When the Wycliffe organization began it focused on Mexico and then Peru, and only with difficulty decided to reach out to the Philippines and beyond. Note also that this new body would try its best to work through existing organizations, but would be willing to engage in "direct activity" where existing organizations did not reach—mentioned again in 63.

64. While it has not been common for Wycliffe to promote Indians as missionaries, Townsend at this early date suggested the importance of Indian work in this light.

82. In the long run, the greatest problem would be to "incite" *existing mission agencies* to reach out to ethnic minorities. But, the new mission must "feel at liberty" to undertake work "where an established agency does not undertake the adequate reaching of the Indians nor care to do so." Note that this came from the committee consisting of Burgess, Townsend and Toms. When the pioneer phase was completed, they would gladly turn this work over to the existing mission agencies—as soon as they "are equipped adequately to carry on the work along the lines laid down."

94. If the bypassing of existing missions was not dangerously revolutionary, the idea of a mission agency be-

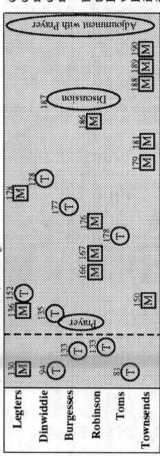

ing run by the missionaries themselves certainly was, at least for the denominational boards. The faith mission movement, by contrast, had a strong element of "field direction" stemming back to the classical home-field struggle which James Hudson Taylor weathered in favor of field control.

110. Presumably the members of the Home Council would be a small number (See paragraph 140, "limited to nine") while the members of the Field Councils would include all missionaries and be more numerous in number, thus assuring the intended "field direction." Wycliffe is distinguished from many mission agencies by the fact that its ultimate authority

derives from active missionaries.

131. Here the hemispheric expanse of their vision is finally confirmed.

135. Having only one field, they began with a General Council that would consist of precisely that field group.

150. Townsend makes a practical motion, pushing things forward.

170. There was certainly a clear idea about the importance of women being involved in the tribal languages since most tribal women knew less Spanish than the men.

172. Missionaries in Guatemala often felt closer to missionaries in China than they did to the people in the U.S.A.. This is not often understood.

173. Hoping that the Indian children could help seed their families with Biblical insights in their mother tongue, the missionary environment obviously still exercised great pressure on the Indians to move into the Spanish language.

177. The issue of direct support versus board support was inevitably raised since the Central American Mission was a Faith Mission involving missionaries who raised their own support while the Presbyterian missionaries were supported indirectly by a salary from the board. The issue was definitely settled in the Faith Mission tradition in paragraph 277.

277. This simple paragraph resolved for the Latin American Indian Mission the question of whether or not to go in the "Faith Mission" direction. (See comment on paragraph 177.) Note that this paragraph was drawn up by Dinwiddie and Mrs. Burgess (see paragraph 178), neither of whom represented the Faith Mission tradition.

Alert activist Townsend made more motions than anyone else, and with his college friend, Robinson, made more than half of all motions.

Comments by Ralph D. Winter
July 1995

References

1. Hugh Steven, *A Thousand Trails; The Personal Journal of William Cameron Townsend, 1917-1919*, (White Rock, British Columbia: Credo Publishing Corporation, 1984), pp. 127-128.
2. *Ibid.*, p. 200.
3. Letter from Elvira Malmstrom to Paul and Dora Burgess, March 2, 1919.
4. Anna Marie Dahlquist, *Burgess of Guatemala*, (Langley, British Columbia: Cedar Books, 1985), p. 67.
5. Paul Burgess, Report on the Sixth Quadrennial International Convention of the Student Volunteer Union at Rochester, New York, 1910.
6. Letter from Paul Burgess to Anna Hertz Burgess, November 29, 1919.
7. Letter from Paul Burgess to Cameron Townsend, August 27, 1920.
8. *Central American Bulletin*, October 15, 1917, p. 6.
9. *Central American Bulletin*, March 15, 1919, p. 11.
10. *Central American Bulletin*, January 15, 1920, p. 13.
11. Letter from A. B. Treichler to Paul and Dora Burgess, January 12, 1921.
12. Letter from Howard Dinwiddie to Paul Burgess, December 14, 1920.
13. Letter from Paul Burgess to Howard Dinwiddie, December 21, 1920.
14. Mildred W. Spain, *And In Samaria*, (Dallas: The Central American Mission, 1954), p. 167.
15. Minutes of the Latin American Indian Mission, January 23-25, 1921.

16. Financial policy of the Latin American Indian Mission

17. Letter from Howard Dinwiddie to Cameron Townsend, April 30, 1921.

18. Letter from Cameron Townsend to Howard Dinwiddie, September 5, 1921.

19. Letter from Cameron Townsend to Howard Dinwiddie, May 16, 1922.

20. *The Sunday School Times*, February 25, 1922.

21. *Ibid.*

22. Letter from Paul Burgess to W. E. McBath, April 9, 1921.

23. *Central American Bulletin*, July 1921, p. 14

24. Letter from L. L. Legters to Paul Burgess, April 7, 1921.

25. Letter from Paul Burgess to L. L. Legters, May 19, 1921.

26. Letter from Howard Dinwiddie to Cameron Townsend, March 24, 1921.

27. Letter from Howard Dinwiddie to Cameron Townsend, June 29, 1921.

28. Letter from Howard Dinwiddie to Cameron Townsend, May 23, 1921.

29. Letter from Stanley White to Paul Burgess, February 16, 1921.

30. Letter from Paul Burgess to Stanley White, March 16, 1921.

31. Letter from Stanley White to Paul Burgess, June 23, 1921.

32. Letter from Edward Bishop to Paul Burgess, June 2, 1920.

33. Letter from Anne McBath to Mary Bishop, May 29, 1921.

34. Letter from Edward Bishop to Howard Dinwiddie, June 9, 1921.

35. Letter from Cameron Townsend to Howard Dinwiddie, September 5, 1921.

36. Letter from Cameron Townsend to Howard Dinwiddie, May 16, 1922.

37. Letter from Luther Rees to Howard Dinwiddie, August 2, 1921.

38. Letter from Howard Dinwiddie to Cameron Townsend, August 23, 1921.

39. Letter from Howard Dinwiddie to Cameron Townsend, May 23, 1921.

40. Letter from Louise Treichler to Paul Burgess, n.d.

41. Letter from Cameron Townsend to Paul Burgess, June 17, 1922.

42. Letter from A. B. Treichler to Paul Burgess, January 28, 1921.

43. Circular letter from Howard Dinwiddie, August 12, 1921.

44. Letter from Howard Dinwiddie to Cameron Townsend, October 4, 1921.
45. Letter from Howard Dinwiddie to Elvira Townsend, 1921.
46. Letter from Paul Burgess to W. E. Robinson, October 22, 1921.
47. Report of the Indian Mission Committee of America, November 28, 1921.
48. Biography of Howard Brooke Dinwiddie, manuscript prepared for *The National Cyclopedia of American Biography*, published by James T. White and Co., New York. From the files of America's Keswick.
49. Letter from Howard Dinwiddie to Luther Rees, October 15, 1921.
50. *The Sunday School Times*, February 25, 1922.
51. Letter from R. H. Young to Paul Burgess, October 11, 1927.
52. Marguerite McQuilkin, *Always in Triumph: The Life of Robert C. McQuilkin*, (New York: Fleming Revell, 1956), p. 67.
53. Circular letter from Brainerd Legters, 1938.
54. Letter from Howard Dinwiddie to Luther Rees, October 15, 1921.
55. Letter from Howard Dinwiddie to Cameron Townsend, June 6, 1922.
56. Letter from A. B. Treichler to Paul Burgess, November 2, 1921.
57. Letter from W. E. Robinson to Paul Burgess, September 6, 1921.
58. Letter from Howard Dinwiddie to Paul Burgess, December 17, 1921.
59. *Ibid.*
60. Letter from Paul Burgess to Rev. and Mrs. S. R. McLaughlin, Febraury 14, 1922.
61. Letter from Albert Hines to Paul Burgess, September 8, 1921.
62. Letter from Cameron Townsend to Howard Dinwiddie, June 20, 1921.
63. Paul Burgess, "Chiapas, a Ripe Field in Mexico," *Missionary Review of the World*, March, 1923, pp. 204-206.
64. *Ibid*, p. 206.
65. Letter from L. L. Legters to Paul Burgess, February 19, 1923.
66. Letter from L. L. Legters to Paul Burgess, March 2, 1923.
67. Letter from L. L. Legters to Paul Burgess, April 24, 1923.
68. *Central American Bulletin*, January, 1922, p. 18.

69. Letter from Cameron Townsend to Howard Dinwiddie, May 16, 1922.

70. Letter from Paul Burgess to Anna Hertz Burgess, June, 1922.

71. *Central American Bulletin,* September, 1922, p. 12.

72. Mildred W. Spain, *And In Samaria,* p. 293.

73. Gonzalo Baez Camargo, *La Evangelización Entre las Razas Indígenas: Apuntes que se someten atentamente a la consideración de los Delegados al Congreso Evangélico de la Habana* (Mexico, 1929), pp. 25-27.

74. Paul Burgess, *Historia de la Obra Evangélica Presbiteriana en Guatemala* (Quezaltenango: El Noticiero Evangélico, 1957), p. 25.

75. Letter from Stanley White to the Guatemala Mission, April 17, 1923.

76. Letter from John Fox to Paul Burgess, February 19, 1917.

77. Letter from Paul Burgess to John Fox, March 17, 1917.

78. *Ibid.*

79. Letter from John Fox to Paul Burgess, November 8, 1917.

80. Letter from Paul Burgess to John Fox, December 14, 1917.

81. Letter from Paul Burgess to Mary Hayberger, November 30, 1922.

82. Letter from Dorothy Peck to Paul and Dora Burgess, November 9, 1927.

83. Letter from Board to Guatemala Mission, March 3, 1937.

84. Edward M. Haymaker, *Footnotes on the Beginnings of the Evangelical Movement in Guatemala* (Guatemala, 1946, Mimeographed edition), p. 57.

85. Wilkins B. Winn, "1894-1896 Arthington Exploration," *CAM Bulletin,* Fall 1981, p. 7.

86. *Ibid.*

87. Letter from Howard Dinwiddie to Lewis Sperry Chafer, June 22, 1923.

88. Letter from L. L. Legters to Karl Hummel, August 16, 1927.

89. Mildred W. Spain, *And In Samaria,* p. 130.

90. Minutes of the Central American Mission, December 19, 1927.

91. Mildred W. Spain, *And In Samaria,* p. 187.

92. Letter from Howard Dinwiddie to Luther Rees, August 1922.

93. *Ibid.*

94. Letter from Luther Rees to Howard Dinwiddie, September 25, 1922.
95. Letter from Frank Toms to Dr. Hummel, n.d.
96. Letter from L. L. Legters to Karl Hummel, November 27, 1934.
97. Letter from Paul Burgess to Cameron Townsend, June 2, 1923.
98. Hugh Milton Coke, Jr., *An Ethnohistory of Bible Translation Among the Maya* (A doctoral dissertation submitted to Fuller Seminary) 1978, p. 342.
99. Paul Burgess, *Historia de la Obra Evangélica Presbiteriana en Guatemala*, p. 45.
100. The Victorious Life Testimony, *In Memory of Howard B. Dinwiddie* (a memorial folder), January 14, 1926.
101. Letter from L. L. Legters to Karl Hummel, January 24, 1927.
102. Aziel W. Jones, *The Holy Spirit's Administration* (Mexico, Ediciones Las Américas, 1978), p. 36.
103. Letter from Thomas Moffett to Paul Burgess, December 27, 1932.
104. Letter from L. L. Legters to Karl Hummel, September 11, 1931.
105. Circular letter from L. L. Legters, September 1, 1933.
106. Circular letter from Edna Legters, February 15, 1934.
107. Letter from Ed Sywulka quoted in *In Other Words*, July/ August 1984.
108. Letter from Brainerd Legters to Paul Burgess, December 3, 1934.
109. Letter from Cameron Townsend to Henry Beets, November 5, 1943.
110. Letter from Howard Dinwiddie to Cameron Townsend, May 23, 1921.

For Further Reading

Burgess, Paul. *Historia de la Obra Evangélica Presbiteriana en Guatemala.* Quezaltenango, Guatemala: El Noticiero Evangélico, 1957.

Cabrera, José, and David Scotchmer, eds. *Apuntes para la Historia: Iglesia Evangélica Nacional Presbiteriana de Guatemala. Historia del Centenario, 1882-1982.* Guatemala: Contendor por La Fe, 1983.

Coke, Hugh Milton, Jr. *An Ethnohistory of Bible Translation Among the Maya.* Doctoral dissertation, Fuller Theological Seminary, 1978.

Dahlquist, Anna Marie. *Burgess of Guatemala.* Langley, British Columbia: Cedar Books, 1985.

Haymaker, Edward M. *Footnotes on the Beginnings of the Evangelical Movement in Guatemala.* Guatemala City, 1946.

Hefley, James and Marti. *Uncle Cam.* Waco, Texas: Word Books, 1974.

Jones, Aziel W. *The Holy Spirit's Administration.* Puebla, Mexico: Ediciones Las Américas, 1978.

Legters, Leonard Livingston. "Disappointments of a Pioneer Missionary." Chapter 13 in *Souls Set Free.* Chicago: The Bible Institute Colportage Association, 1929.

McQuilkin, Marguerite. *Always in Triumph: The Life of Robert C. McQuilkin.* New York: Fleming Revell, 1956.

Martin, Dorothy. *100 .. And Counting: A Centennial History of CAM International.* Dallas, Texas: CAM International, 1990.

Scotchmer, David G. *Symbols of Salvation: Interpreting Highland Maya Protestants in Context* (A doctoral dissertation submitted to State University of New York), 1991.

Scotchmer, David G. "Called for Life: The Literary Contribution of Edward M. Haymaker to an Ethnohistory of Protestant Missionary Ideology, Guatemala, 1887-1947." In *Missionaries, Anthropologists, and Cultural Change: Studies in Third World Societies # 25,* edited by Vinson Sutlive et. al., College of William and Mary, pp. 323-368.

Spain, Mildred W. *And In Samaria.* Dallas: The Central American Mission, 1954.

Steven, Hugh. *A Thousand Trails; The Personal Journal of William Cameron Townsend, 1917-1919.* White Rock, British Columbia: Credo Publishing Corporation, 1984.

Wallis, Ethel Emily, and Bennett, Mary Angela. *Two Thousand Tongues to Go: The Story of the Wycliffe Bible Translators.* New York: Harper and Brothers, 1959.

Zapata, Virgilio A. *Historia de la Iglesia Evangélica en Guatemala.* Guatemala City, 1982.